RECONNECT

EXPERIENCING DEEPER INTIMACY WITH GOD

JOAN E. MURRAY

Book cover designed by, Woodson Creative Studio.

Joan Murray Ministries & Seeds Of Hope Worldwide Missions

26340 FM 1736

Waller, TX 77848

281-398-2501

PRAISE FOR RECONNECT

"Reconnect" is Joan Murray's fourteenth book and a literary gem from this accomplished author. Joan echoes a heartfelt cry to the body of Christ, as that of a modern-day John the Baptist: 'Return to the Lord'. She gives a compelling challenge to believers, young and old, to examine their relationship with the Lord and their level of intimacy with him.

"Reconnect" deals with the center of our spiritual personality, the heart, with utmost candor. Joan is brilliant in how she not only describes the various potential problems with the heart but gives the believer step-by-step solutions to a happier, healthier heart that brings pleasure to the Lord.

You will discover "Reconnect" to be an expedient instrument of your spiritual toolbox. The principles herein are timeless and designed to be revisited frequently. When applied, these virtues can keep your heart focused on God's initial plan to have ongoing fellowship with His most incredible creation, man, while enjoying the full benefits thereof.

WE ARE grateful for the opportunity to have read and learn from the wisdom imparted by Joan. From the moment we began digesting "Reconnect," we uncovered areas in our own lives in need of rekindling toward the essence of God. We pray this book exposes anything in your life that is preventing you from experiencing the highest level of intimacy with our Father through our Lord Jesus Christ.

Pastors Jermaine & Ericka White
OneChurch
Tampa, Florida

"RECONNECT" has come from the heart of the Father and is a charge to live out of our highest call -- fellowship with God. God's vision is not primarily our ministry assignment or what we do for Him; it is about our relationship with Him. It is wholehearted lovers of God with hearts overflowing with love toward God and others. This book tackles the greatest issues in the church today -- Are our hearts tender toward God? How deeply do we love Him? What is hindering love?

GOD WANTS to remove all the issues that hinder love, but we must partner with Him in the place of cultivation. If we do our part, He will do His part. If we work the ground, He will tenderize our hearts, transform us, and bring forth fruit and maturity in us.

IF THE THOUGHT of Jesus does not stir the human heart with burning desire for Him, we need to check our drift. To sail in an ocean and never check your drift is foolishness. A one-degree drift in the ocean left unchecked could cause you to miss a continent. That goes for our hearts being connected to God also. Receiving the wisdom of God in this book should challenge us all to check our drift, to check our heart condition, and to reconnect with the God of Burning Desire and live fully alive in the love of God!

> Pastors Randy & Jennifer Campbell
> Mosaic House of Prayer
> Katy, Texas

WHEN A HOUSEHOLD ITEM isn't working properly, the first thing I check is if the electrical plug is firmly connected to the outlet. When our spiritual walk seems powerless, we should check to make sure our heart is connected fully to Christ.

JOAN MURRAY'S BOOK "RECONNECT" is a "must read" for any Christian experiencing a season of duty or dryness. This book lays out a clear path to a deeper relationship with Jesus. Joan lays out a thorough schematic diagram in "Reconnect" on how to keep the Holy Spirit's power flowing through us and into the lives of others. She lovingly challenges those who might think their "connection" is OK to remember what Paul warned in his letter to the Corinthians, "So, if you think you are standing, be careful you don't fall."

AS A TEACHER, Joan instructs with clarity and biblical soundness; as a speaker, she encourages the church to walk in power and victory; and, as a mentor, she inspires others to dig deep into the Truth of God's Word and follow hard after Jesus. We recommend this book to keep you connected or help you reconnect to God's power source.

Tim & Polly Barker, Lead Pastors
Katy Community Fellowship
Katy, Texas

It is a great joy and privilege to share my thoughts on this powerful book, "Reconnect, Experiencing Deeper Intimacy with God." James 4:8 said draw nigh to God, and he will draw nigh to you. In order to have a deeper relationship with God, one must long for him, thirst for him, and hunger for him. Chapter one of this great book talks about our disconnection. Being disconnected from God can cause your love to grow cold, your light to go dim, and your life to become unfruitful. After a believer becomes disconnected from God, they begin to have a heart issue -- lack of confidence in God's word; lack of perseverance during trials; lack of prayer, fellowship, and bible reading; lack of witnessing -- which then allows the devil to blind their minds.

Having a heart of a servant will make us eager to take a public stand for Christ. It was once said, "If you don't stand for something you will fall for anything." A true servant of God who has a servant's heart will desire true devotion with God. Jesus said in Matt: 15:8, but their heart is far from me. A heart of a servant is not merely feelings, nor is it a passing emotion. It is an act of respect and loyalty to God. A committed and dedicated heart is a heart that loves God. God is looking for saved men and women with a true heart for God, His Word, the House of God, and the people of God.

THIS BOOK, "RECONNECT," will touch many hearts to be reconnected back to God. My prayers for myself and those who will read this wonderful book is we will always stay connected to God throughout our lives. The benefits of reconnecting are: One will gain a heart of trust, a heart of humility, a heart of courage, a yielded heart, and a heart that will be open to God. Last, but not least, I thank God for this powerful, inspirational woman of God, Joan Murray, who has influenced my life and for this anointed book that is needed for this end time season.

Pastors Booker & Rose Hale
Free At Last Praise and Worship Center
Humble, Texas

ACKNOWLEDGEMENTS

I thank the Lord Jesus Christ for His inspiration, leadership, and guidance in writing this book. With His help, I examined my heart and assessed what work was needed in my own life so the message of this book would touch the hearts of those who needed to reconnect with Him. I am eternally grateful for His love and compassion toward me.

I thank my Board of Directors and the Joan Murray Ministries Team for their continued support, encouragement, and prayer each time I undertake another assignment to write the words the Lord gives me.

My sincere thanks to Pastors Rudy and Anne Marie Beltran, Pastors Tim and Polly Barker, Pastors Jermaine and Ericka White, Pastors Booker and Rose Hale, and Pastors

Randy and Jennifer Campbell for their time and commitment to reading and endorsing this book.

To a great team of editors - Phyllis Villanueva, Julia Rigos, and Michelle Flippins, you have helped me make this project what God intended it to be. My sincere thanks to Daniel Leal for the beautiful book cover.

To my family and friends, thanks for your prayers, encouragement, and excitement each time God gives me an assignment to write a new book.

Thanks to the faithful supporters of Joan Murray Ministries for your prayers, seeds, time, and labor of love with me in dispensing the Gospel of the Kingdom.

CONTENTS

FOREWARD

I first heard of Joan Murray after some of the ladies from our church returned from a women's conference in Houston. While in Houston, they attended Joan's bible study; and, as soon as they got back, they highly recommended I invite her to do a workshop at our church.

I took their advice; and, after meeting Joan and listening to her teach the Word of God, I knew the Lord was establishing a kingdom connection. Since that time, our church has had the honor of hosting Joan multiple times every year as a speaker to provide training to our volunteers and key leaders.

As you get to know Joan, you quickly learn she is wholeheartedly devoted to her relationship with God and has dedicated her life to kingdom and advancement. Joan is a mighty woman of faith who is focused on her calling -- first and foremost to be an example of Christ then to fulfill the assignment of God upon her life. She is an excellent teacher and communicator, and she is passionate about helping people find freedom and victory in a growing relationship with God.

As I read through the pages of her latest work "Reconnect," I found myself reflecting and searching my own heart to see what areas of my life were keeping me from enjoying deeper intimacy with God. After all, the greatest blessing in life is not some temporary possession or success but instead we can know our Creator, God, intimately.

This powerful truth—we, as mere men, might know the omnipotent and infinite almighty God—transcends the finite human mind and invigorates the human soul. In Colossians 1 we read, "He (Christ) is the image of the invisible God, the firstborn over all creation. For by Him all things were created: things in heaven and on earth, visible and invisible, whether thrones or powers or rulers or authorities; all things were created by Him and for Him. He is before all things, and in Him all things hold together." The invisible God, creator of heaven and earth, made himself known to mankind in the person of Jesus Christ; and, today, people like you and me have the indescribable opportunity to have fellowship with the Creator.

These are the very words Christ prayed before His final ascension, "Now this is eternal life: that they may know you, the only true God, and Jesus Christ, whom you have sent." (John 17:3). Through a relationship with Christ, every person on the face of the earth has a chance to know their Maker. What I have learned in my time as a pastor is this amazing and profound truth sometimes loses its power and significance in the life of a believer.

In "Reconnect," Joan will help you assess your relationship with God and, more specifically, the condition of your heart. She will ask you honest questions to help you identify any areas of your life that have caused you to lose connection with the heart of God. Whether you are a new believer or have been a believer for many years "Reconnect" is going to challenge you and enable you to experience the remarkable blessing of deeper intimacy with God.

Rudy Beltran
Founder and Pastor
Destiny Through Christ Church

INTRODUCTION

I n writing this book, I considered some people would look at the title and instantly decide they are not disconnected from God. Some would argue their relationship with God is intact and does not need a reconnection.

Sometimes this most crucial relationship needs a tune-up despite how intimate we believe our relationship is with God. Throughout our walk with God, we encounter challenges that test our devotion to Him. These challenges will cause some of us to deviate from His narrow path. Often, the change is so subtle we do not realize we are not where we think we are in our walk. As a result, we may not be as committed, trustworthy, and faithful as we once were.

A tune-up is necessary because it allows us to stop and evaluate where we are in our faith walk. As you take the time to examine your heart, you will unearth issues that are keeping you from the level of connection you desire to have with God.

We all have issues of the heart that need to be fixed. Two of our most significant problems are how tender our hearts are toward God and how deeply we love Him. Conduct a self-examination for me. When you think of Jesus, does your heart overflow with love for Him? Does it still melt when you think about what He has done for you? Do you remember how you felt when He first saved and radically changed your life? Do you still feel awe and adoration as when you first encountered Him? It is sad to say, but many of us are no longer moved because we have become so used to hearing about Him and seeing various movies about His sacrifice. Some of us have become very complacent in our relationship with God.

Adam and Eve also became complacent in their relationship with God. They took their daily face-to-face meetings with Him for granted. Because they did not guard their intimate fellowship with Him, the enemy could separate them from God. I venture to say Adam and Eve did not realize what they were about to lose when they allowed the enemy to seduce them. Only after God evicted them from the garden did they recognize the great price they had paid for their disobedience. They lost their intimate fellowship with their Creator. What a deep emptiness this must have left in their hearts.

This book, Reconnect, challenges us to look at our hearts and relationship with God. It dares to ask difficult questions about our heart condition, commitment, dedication, trustworthiness, and humility. Reconnect pushes us to examine whether we are walking on the narrow path that leads to life or veering onto the broad path that leads only to destruction (Matthew 7:13-14). There are many benefits of having a deep intimate relationship with God. When you and I decide to give all our heart to Him, we will experience the fullness of life.

If you feel you already have a deep connection to God, I still challenge you to read this book and ask yourself at the end of each chapter if there is room for growth and improvement. I believe, like me, you will come to see a more profound intimacy is still needed in your relationship with God. Therefore, dive deeply into the pages of this book and discover some keys that will bring about greater closeness to your Creator. I encourage you to go deeper in your intimacy with God so your joy will overflow.

Joan E. Murray
Founder
Joan Murray Ministries
Seeds of Hope Worldwide Missions

OTHER BOOKS BY:
JOAN E. MURRAY

Boldness in Christ

Broken, Yet Unstoppable

Called and Chosen for Destiny

Discovering God Vol. 1

Discovering God Vol. 2

Faith That Conquers

Flow Through Me, Lord

Freedom In The Son

Hope In Difficult Seasons

I MUST PRAY

Lord, Make Me Whole

Overcoming Loneliness and Aloneness

Reconnect

Señor, Hazme Íntegro

Show Me How to Love
Time in Life's Waiting Room
Winning In The Battles of Life
Worship, Our Deepest Need
You Can TRUST Him

CHAPTER 1
DISCONNECTED

Early one evening, the voice of God rang out in the Garden of Eden, "Adam, where are you," God called. Adam answered, "I heard You in the garden, and I was afraid because I was naked, so I hid myself." Adam had an intimate relationship with his Creator from the first moment of his existence—he walked and talked with God in the cool of each day—until this day.

When God came looking for Adam for their face-to-face fellowship, He could not find him in the usual spot. Adam hid from God because he had become disconnected. He was naked, ashamed, and lost, and for the first time in his existence, Adam hid from the One who meant everything to him.

As you continue reading, you will discover how the devil

tricked Adam into losing his connection with God and how he also has a plan for your demise.

Now the serpent was craftier than any of the wild animals the LORD God had made. He said to the woman, "Did God really say, 'You must not eat from the tree in the garden'?" The woman said to the serpent, "We may eat fruit from the trees in the garden, but God did say, 'You must not eat fruit from the tree that is in the middle of the garden, and you must not touch it, or you will die.'" "You will not surely die," the serpent said to the woman. "For God knows that when you eat of it your eyes will be opened, and you will be like God, knowing good and evil." When the woman saw that the fruit of the tree was good for food and pleasing to the eye, and also desirable for gaining wisdom, she took some and ate it. She also gave some to her husband, who was with her, and he ate it. Then the eyes of both of them were opened, and they realized they were naked; so they sewed fig leaves together and made coverings for themselves. Then the man and his wife heard the sound of the LORD God as he was walking in the garden in the cool of the day, and they hid from the Lord God among the trees of the garden. But the LORD God called to the man, "Where are you?" He answered, "I heard you in the garden, and I was afraid because I was naked; so I hid." And he said, "Who told you that you were naked? Have you eaten from the tree that I commanded you not to eat from?" The man said, "The woman you put here with me – she gave me some fruit from the tree, and I ate it." Then the LORD God said to the woman, "What is this you have done?" The woman said, "The serpent deceived me, and I ate."
—Genesis 3:1-13 (NIV)

Hum. There was trouble in the Garden of Eden because the devil plotted and planned the demise of Adam and Eve, and he succeeded. He wanted their authority and power, and he won because they missed something significant in God's instructions. In their desire to be like God and to know what He knows, they did not realize they already had God's power and authority. They had the nature and mind of God, were created in His image, and had access to all the power they could handle. Satan came to kill, steal, and destroy them (to make them powerless). He succeeded (John 10:10). The enemy is determined to cause a disconnection between you and God, and it is your responsibility to withstand Satan and overcome him.

When I hear the word reconnect, it speaks to me of having a prior connection to something or someone—a connection that is now broken. Reconnect means to link up. God created man to connect and fellowship with Him. This connection was to ensure our success; therefore, the instruction God gave Adam not to eat from the one tree in the garden was not meant to keep him from enjoying himself but to keep him safe.

In my book, *Winning in the Battles of Life,* I discuss how God gave Adam the instruction before He created Eve. This account tells us Satan must have been in the garden because he repeated to Eve—almost verbatim —what God had told Adam. The devil did not approach Adam to cause man's downfall; he spoke to the woman. God talked to Adam, the head of the family, but the enemy bypassed him and spoke to Eve. He made her doubt herself and caused her to question

God's instructions to her husband. The devil tempted her through her physical senses. She wanted what her eyes saw, what her flesh cried out for, and what pride told her she had to have because it looked good, would taste good, and would certainly make her feel good. Her desire was so over-whelming she did not stop to consider God's instruction that if they ate from the tree, they would die. Eve did not under-stand death and made her decision without considering the consequences.

Now, this is where the story gets more interesting. After Eve took and ate the fruit, the Bible says she gave it to her husband, who was with her. I have a question. Was Adam standing right there as the enemy enticed Eve? Yes, he was. He heard the devil convince his wife to sin and disobey God, and he neither said nor did anything to stop the exchange even though he had received explicit instructions from the Lord. Some believe Eve did not need to look for Adam to share the fruit as he was next to her. She turned and handed the fruit to him, and Adam ate without being coerced. Adam willingly and willfully ate the fruit.

I WOULD VENTURE to say once Adam saw that Eve had eaten the fruit and was still alive, he decided to join her because he was not about to lose his connection with her. Maybe he also wanted to discover what she had experi-enced from eating the fruit. Adam chose death and separa-tion from God so he could stay connected to Eve, and he chose Eve and disobedience instead of God and obedience to His Word. Disconnection happened immediately. Their eyes were opened, and they instantly knew what sin was.

For the first time, they noticed their nakedness and were ashamed.

THE FULL REALIZATION of their actions came to light later that evening. God came to visit Adam and Eve as He had done all along. God knew they had sinned but still came to see them because they were His children. God had to deal with their disobedience and the devil who caused the disconnection with His children. When God asked Adam where he was, God was not asking about his physical location in the Garden of Eden. God was asking about his heart condition and spiritual location. Adam's nakedness brought shame, and his disobedience resulted in fear causing him to hide from God. God, in His great love and compassion, killed one of the animals Adam had named to provide clothing for them. Sin caused the first shedding of blood.

As God revealed the consequences of their sins and the suffering they would endure, Adam and Eve learned the true meaning of death and how disconnected they were from God. I imagine Adam thought He would continue daily fellowship with God after God's visit, but God's presence was removed from him. When Adam experienced total disconnection, he finally understood what death was. Death meant he was separated from God, and God would no longer meet with him face-to-face.

WHEN GOD asked them what they had done, He allowed them to own their sins, repent, turn away from disobedience, and turn back to God. However, Adam blamed Eve, and Eve blamed the serpent. Neither of them acknowledged their wrongdoing. Disconnection happened not only with God but also in their relationship with each other because the enemy caused them to start playing the blame game. Many centuries later, we are still experiencing this same disconnection from God and one another. People are still blaming others for their sins. Because of Adam and Eve's disconnection, our connection with God was broken. You and I needed to reconnect to the heart of God, and He provided the way.

ADAM MISSED his opportunity to stay connected to God, but Jesus, known as the second Adam, did not. The devil knew Jesus had fasted and prayed for forty days when he went to Jesus in the desert and told Him to turn stone into bread. Jesus replied, "Man shall not live on bread alone" (Luke 4:4 NIV). This temptation came when Jesus was hungry and at a weak and vulnerable point in His life. The devil tempted Jesus with food, tried to get Him to test God, and offered Him the kingdoms of the world and their splendor. Jesus responded to each temptation with the Word of God.

THE DEVIL THOUGHT Jesus would succumb to His fleshly desires as Adam and Eve had. He did not understand Jesus was an obedient Son. We, too, must become obedient sons and daughters of God. Jesus spoke the Word of God to the devil, and the devil had to flee. Speaking the Word of God to the devil is one of the most potent weapons we have at our disposal to defeat him.

You may be disconnected from God and His perfect plan for your life, but you can return to Him today. As you journey through this book, I invite you to examine the areas of your life that may have caused you to become estranged from the heart of God. Decide today to reestablish the connection by plugging into your Source of power—God.

CHAPTER 2
A HEART ISSUE

Adam and Eve experienced a disconnection from God because they had a heart issue. Instead of longing after God, they longed after something else.

When Adam and Eve turned their hearts away from God, they thought they were attaining something more significant than they already had in their relationship with Him. To their dismay, they discovered nothing could compare to fellowship with God. We also lose our connection with God when we have issues in our hearts that we do not allow God to address or process. These issues affect our relationship and fellowship with God and cause us not to understand that whatever affects our hearts will affect our entire lives.

LOOKING BACK OVER YOUR LIFE, can you see where you got off track? Something was born in your mind that later affected your heart and caused you to make the wrong choice, severely affecting your life in some cases. At first, the choice seemed simple and non-evasive. Feeling that you could manage, you took the plunge without realizing you had stepped into a trap designed for your defeat. When Eve first saw the fruit God had told them not to eat, it appealed to her and seemed harmless. In her heart, she reasoned there could be no harm in tasting it. The more Eve thought about the mystery of what God had said a desire birthed in her heart to be like God and to know what He knows. She never saw the danger signs or the pitfalls. She missed hearing the warning bells by focusing exclusively on what she sensed and wanted.

Like Eve, we get so focused on the things we want we never see the danger signs. All we see is a light that beckons us. Isn't it interesting how the enemy can make things seem appealing to our senses? We encounter problems when our hearts long after the wrong things. The right desires that should motivate us toward the right choices are often hidden, and what we do not want to do are the things that keep resurfacing.

In a recent counseling session, I spoke to a gentleman who shared his struggles as he attempted to do what was right. He said he knows that stealing is wrong, and the pull to do wrong is stronger than the desire to do right. He longs to make the right decisions, but it is easier for him to do the wrong thing. He feared he could not change midstream and start doing what was right after years of following the wrong motivations of his heart. The Apostle Paul explained the man's struggle in Romans 7.

So I DISCOVER THIS PRINCIPLE: when I want to do good, evil is with me. For in my inner self I joyfully agree with God's law. But I see a different law in the parts of my body, waging war against the law of my mind and taking me prisoner to the law of sin in the parts of my body. What a wretched man I am! Who will rescue me from this body of death? I thank God through Jesus Christ our Lord! So then, with my mind I myself am a slave to the law of God, but with my flesh, to the law of sin.
—Romans 7:21-25 (CSB)

PAUL WAS STRUGGLING against his fleshly desires. He wanted to do what was right, but evil thoughts and desires were always present. He knew his weaknesses and was not satisfied with the results he was producing. Paul recognized the evil influences that motivated him. He fought and persevered to be honorable and did not allow wrong motives to overtake his life. I can picture him after he sinned, calling to God for help and deliverance from the prison of sinful desires. Paul understood the struggles you and I would face as we try to keep our hearts pure before the Lord. He wrestled with his demons and many temptations but did not allow those roadblocks to stop him from fulfilling his purpose.

As YOU WRESTLE with unwholesome thoughts, remember these things are designed to keep you from bearing the good fruit in your life. Make the decision not to give up or submit to them. Your struggles are against the demonic influences that are all around you. The enemy went directly into Eve's presence to entice her away from God's plans.

Today, he whispers in our ears and tells us the temptation we surrender to will not harm us. He wants you to believe there is nothing wrong with your unwholesome desires. Ask yourself, "Is this God's best for me?" The devil has said some of you were born for this and that God understands how it is. He is a liar trying to trick you away from the loving protection of your Father. The devil has a corrupt heart. He served in heaven as the praise and worship leader but wanted to be like the Most High God and ascend to God's throne. He wanted to be praised and worshipped, so God threw him out of heaven. Now the devil's full-time job is to tempt you to cause corruption in your heart and disconnect you from the heart of God.

The heart issues are about how intensely you and I love God. Is our love for God so intense we are willing to fight and overcome wrong desires to stay in close communion with Him? God has much to say about our hearts.

Heart Check

The good man brings good things out of the good stored up in his heart, and the evil man brings evil things out of the evil stored up in his heart. For out of the overflow of his heart his mouth speaks.
—Luke 6:45 (NIV)

Keep thy heart with all diligence; for out of it are the issues of life.
—Proverbs 4:23 (KJV)

But what comes out of the mouth proceeds from the heart, and this defiles a person.
—Matthew 15:18 (ESV)

For where your treasure is, there your heart will be also.
—Luke 12:34 (NIV)

For now we see through a glass, darkly; but then face to face: now I know in part; but then shall I know even as also I am known.
—1 Corinthians 13:12 (KJV)

As you can see from these scriptures, the problems start with our hearts; we have heart issues that must be fixed. When you have good stored in your heart, you will live a productive life with good results. To hold good in your heart, you make a conscious decision to do what is right no matter how you feel or how enticing the temptations may be. Doing what is right is not a decision you make only once; it is a decision you must make daily. Sometimes you must make this decision numerous times a day to produce the right results. At times, you may have to stop and remind the enemy who you are, that you belong to Christ, and you only choose to think and meditate on those things which are pure, lovely, and have a good report (Philippians 4:8).

Only you can keep your heart pure, and you must be diligent about it. You must guard what you allow to enter your heart through your eye and ear gates. What you allow to enter will corrupt your heart or bring blessings to your life.

The Bible says out of our hearts flow the issues of life. What problems are you having? They come from a heart that does not have the right ingredients to produce the correct results. Are you having a problem with your flesh? Check your heart. Are you having an issue with unstable emotions? Check your heart. Are you having an issue with unwholesome desires? Check what you allow to penetrate your heart because whatever you allow will birth these desires and bear the wrong fruit in your life. Whatever your issues, they flow or spring forth out of your heart. No one can severely guard your heart but you, with the Holy Spirit, and you must allow Him access.

WHAT IS YOUR GREATEST TREASURE? Is it something you hold close to your heart? Is it something you do not like to share with others? Does this treasure keep you from giving to those in need? We can hold on to our treasure so tightly we do not allow the Holy Spirit to dwell and reign freely in us.

LUKE 12:34 says your heart will be where your treasure is. Anything that has your heart will ultimately control your life. So, if the wrong treasure has your heart, it will produce sinful desires in you. Your greatest treasure needs to be God's greatest treasure, and your heart will always produce good fruit when it becomes God's greatest treasure.

WHAT DO you think God's greatest treasure is? You, of course! When Jesus came to earth and died, He did not die for what has become our treasures (e.g., money, position, popularity, houses, cars, etc.). He came for only one treasure —people.

Jesus says, *"But we have this treasure in earthen vessels, that the Excellency of the power may be of God, and not of us."*
—2 Corinthians 4:7 (KJV)

WHEN GOD looks at His treasure, He sees you! You are one of His earthen vessels created in His image. You are His finest masterpiece. Jesus left His splendor, majesty, and worship to die for you because you are God's treasure. God has poured His excellence and power into you so you may understand He is the one who empowers you for greatness. Allow your most remarkable treasure to be Him. Let Him become the most significant issue of your heart so He can flow out of you to impact the hearts and lives of the people around you. Give God full access to your heart and life, and watch as He reveals His treasure (you) to the world.

WHAT DO you see when you take a close look at your life? Do you see your heart clearly, or is your view dark and cloudy? According to 1 Corinthians 13:12, we see through a dark glass; we do not see all that is in our hearts. We sometimes deceive ourselves by believing we have a good heart and are doing what is right. We think all is well with us and in our world, and it is at times; but at other times, it is not. If you take the time to search your heart, you will find hidden things that are not a reflection of the Christ whom you serve.

WHILE IN COLLEGE, I worked in retail and learned something valuable that I have used ever since. Each year, we would take inventory of the merchandise to account for what was missing or damaged in the store. I realize we should do a heart check inventory of our lives regularly to see what needs to be purified in our souls. So, each birthday, I review my year to see in which areas I have grown, how effective I have been in serving God, how many lives I have impacted for His glory, and the things I have accomplished. I also look at the areas where I was deficient and ineffective in my Christian walk. I do an honest inventory of my life to see the areas that need improvement.

When I look at myself, I ask the Lord to help me see clearly and reveal my heart's hidden secrets and treasures. I then journal my findings and list what I want to accomplish and improve during the following year. I review my list yearly to see my accomplishments and what I did not complete and devise an improvement plan for next year. This inventory helps keep my heart in check and causes me to grow in my Christian walk. Mostly it is joyful to review my list, but sometimes I say, "Ouch," because I have missed something significant in my walk. When that happens, I remember Romans chapter eight says there is no condemnation for those who are in Christ Jesus.

When I mess up, I repent and ask God to help me do better, and He always does. I invite you to do your own heart check inventory so God can be glorified through you.

EVEN JESUS WENT through testing and trials to examine His heart to see if it was right toward God for the fulfillment of His assignment. When He was tempted in the wilderness,

Jesus proved His heart was indeed right and fulfilled all He had to accomplish. When He came face-to-face with the devil, Jesus defeated him because His heart was pure and steadfast toward God (Matthew 4:1-11).

Do you have a specific heart issue that needs to be addressed? Allow the Lord to deal with it, so He can get you back on track to your destiny. One of my favorite heart-check prayers is Psalm 51, and I pray it also becomes one of your favorite heart-check prayers as you seek to please the Lord.

HAVE MERCY ON ME, O God, according to your unfailing love; according to your great compassion blot out my transgressions. Wash away all my iniquity and cleanse me from my sin. For I know my transgressions, and my sin is always before me. Against you, you only, have I sinned and done what is evil in your sight; so you are right in your verdict and justified when you judge. Surely I was sinful at birth, sinful from the time my mother conceived me. Yet you desired faithfulness even in the womb; you taught me wisdom in that secret place. Cleanse me with hyssop, and I will be clean; wash me, and I will be whiter than snow. Let me hear joy and gladness; let the bones you have crushed rejoice. Hide your face from my sins and blot out all my iniquity. Create in me a pure heart, O God, and renew a steadfast spirit within me. Do not cast me from your presence or take your Holy Spirit from me. Restore to me the joy of your salvation and grant me a willing spirit, to sustain me. Then I will teach transgressors your ways, so that sinners will turn back to you. Deliver me from the guilt of bloodshed, O God, you who are God my Savior, and my tongue will sing of your righteousness. Open my lips, Lord, and my mouth will declare your praise. You do not delight in sacrifice, or I would bring it; you do not take pleasure in burnt offerings. My sacrifice, O God, is a broken spirit; a broken and contrite heart you, God, will not despise. May it please you to prosper Zion, to build up the walls of Jerusalem. Then you will delight in the sacrifices of the righteous, in burnt offerings offered whole; then bulls will be offered on your altar.

—Psalm 51:1-19 (NIV)

IN THE UPCOMING CHAPTERS, I will address the areas of our hearts that need reconnecting to God. As we study together, I challenge you to examine the following: your servanthood, commitment, dedication, trustworthiness, humility, courage, yieldedness, and whether you have unveiled your heart before God. After a thorough examination, you will discover the great benefits of reconnecting to God, your Source for everything that pertains to life and godliness. If you are ready for some great discoveries, **Let's Go!**

CHAPTER 3
HEART OF A SERVANT

 *Faithfulness is the foundation for every person who has the heart of a servant.*

In those days when the number of disciples was increasing, the Grecian Jews among them complained against the Hebraic Jews because their widows were being overlooked in the daily distribution of food. So the Twelve gathered all the disciples together and said, "It would not be right for us to neglect the ministry of the word of God in order to wait on tables. Brothers, choose seven men from among you who are known to be full of the Spirit and wisdom. We will turn this responsibility over to them and will give our attention to prayer and the ministry of the word. This proposal pleased the whole group. They chose Stephen, a man full of faith and of the Holy Spirit. Now Stephen, a man full of God's grace and power, did great wonders and miraculous signs among the people.
—Acts 6:1-5, 8 (NIV)

I N THE ABOVE SCRIPTURE, the disciples realized they could not take care of the needs of the people and still be effective in dispensing the word of the Lord, so they chose seven men to carry out these duties. Of the seven men chosen, Stephen had the anointing of God upon his life. He stood out among the others, not only for his level of service but also for his faithfulness. God used him significantly to demonstrate His power to the Israeli people.

STEPHEN WAS A MAN, who had an intimate relationship with God, and it showed in everything he did. Even though he was called to help minister to the needs of the people by serving them, God's power was visible in his life as he worked, as it was in the lives of the disciples. Stephen's name means crown, and he was indeed a crown—a visible testimony to who Jesus truly is. Stephen operated in two significant roles in his calling. He was a deacon who helped the needy widows and orphans when the city authorities no longer provided for them because of their declared faith in Jesus Christ. He was also an evangelist who was extremely bold in his faith. Stephen walked in the power of God and, as a result, performed great signs and wonders among the believers.

Outside of his calling to serve people, he focused on reaching the lost for Christ. Having studied the law and the Word of God, he had many heated debates with the religious Jews who could not refute his preaching and the truths he declared. When they became angry at him and plotted to take his life, Stephen kept serving with a heart to please God.

Even during his trials, Stephen was committed and faithful to his call. He was entrusted with responsibilities and performed them at the highest level. He served where he was assigned and demonstrated dependability and faithfulness. He was constant in his devotion to God and the people. Stephen never wavered from his calling; he served with commitment and passion by giving his all to Jesus Christ. Stephen had the heart of a servant, like Jesus, and he modeled a true example of the Savior.

As we examine Stephen's life, we will see how closely he resembled Christ. His life was a living example that people could view and follow. As you and I examine ourselves, we must consider whether or not people can see servanthood stamped in our hearts and follow our examples. Do you serve with passion and commitment? Are you faithful to the assignments you have been given? Can you be trusted to follow through? As you answer these questions, examine your heart and ask God to show you if you genuinely serve Him with all you have. To experience a deep connection to God and develop an even deeper intimacy with Him, you must search your heart to discover if you truly have the heart to serve Him and others.

A Heart Like Christ

Our heart is the substance or core of who we are. Our heart is our inner being and has nothing to do with our external self. It is the seat of our desires, emotions, intellect, mind, passion, and wills. What is in our hearts motivates and propels us to do things that follow God's will for our lives.

GOD looks at our hearts and blesses and promotes us based on what He finds there. Do you have the heart to please Him and bless the lives of people? When God looks at your heart, does He find Himself stamped all over it, or is your heart so crowded with worldly things that a search has to be conducted to see if God is living in any portion of it?

STEPHEN DISCOVERED the secret to a life that pleases God. He was loving, caring, and compassionate; his heart was sincere and pure. Like Jesus, Stephen was concerned about the needs of the people. God desires His people to live strong, healthy, and abundant lives. He never leaves people in the broken condition in which He finds them. During a crisis, He always steps in and brings wholeness and healing to all who desire to be well. Because Stephen had a similar heart for the needs of broken people, God used him to impact many.

IN ACTS 7, Stephen delivered a speech to the Sanhedrin council that left them speechless. He started with God appearing to Abraham and told the story in its entirety up to the death of Jesus. Stephen intended to show them Jesus was the Son of God whom God had sent to save His people; however, their hearts were not open to receive the truth. He called them stiff-necked people with uncircumcised hearts and ears. Stephen sounded like Jesus! He told them they were like their fathers, who had always resisted the power and presence of the Holy Spirit. He reminded them that their fathers persecuted all the prophets God had sent to help them and killed those who predicted the coming of the Righteous One. Stephen challenged them with the truth that they had murdered Jesus because, like their fathers, they refused to believe and obey the law.

STEPHEN WAS BOLD AND TENACIOUS; he did not back down even though he realized his words would have grave consequences. He spoke boldly to the Israelites as Jesus did and was not afraid to die for what he believed. Stephen poured out his heart to the people, and as he gave them a history lesson, he peeled back the religious masks they had hidden behind for centuries. Their masks kept them from examining themselves, seeing their sins, and recognizing they were in desperate need of the Savior. Stephen revealed the people to themselves and caused them to see what was in their hearts. He clearly showed them what they looked like with the religious covering they wore. He exposed their humanness and revealed the intentions of their hearts. The truth was so pointed it infuriated them. He showed them the heart condition that was hidden behind their religious masks, a heart condition that led them to kill Jesus. Although this truth cost Stephen his life, he never took his focus off the Savior.

Staying Focused

JESUS SAID, "No one who puts a hand to the plow and looks back is fit for service in the kingdom of God" (Luke 9:62 NIV). Stephen focused on his walk with Jesus and stayed the course because he understood there was no turning back once he put his hands on the plow. The Scripture uses the example of a farmer plowing his field. The farmer knew he had to stay focused and not look behind him or else he would get off course and plow crooked lines.

STEPHEN PUT his hands on the plow and raced toward the destiny God had for him. He accepted his assignment willingly, even in the face of death. Stephen was focused on his course and did not take his eyes off the One who saved him. He set his face like flint and boldly told the story of Jesus Christ, whom the Jews had crucified.

STEPHEN UNDERSTOOD he had a destiny and was determined not to miss it. He raced toward his destiny with determination and boldness and embraced all God assigned to him. Stephen fulfilled his destiny by boldly facing the enemies of Jesus Christ and speaking the truth to them.

"And now you have betrayed and murdered him - you who have received the law that was put into effect through angels, but have not obeyed it. When they heard this, they were furious and gnashed their teeth at him. But Stephen, full of the Holy Spirit, looked up to heaven and saw the glory of God, and Jesus standing at the right hand of God. "Look," he said, "I see heaven open and the Son of Man standing at the right hand of God." At this they covered their ears and, yelling at the top of their voices, they all rushed at him, dragged him out of the city and began to stone him. Meanwhile, the witnesses laid their clothes at the feet of a young man named Saul. While they were stoning him, Stephen prayed, "Lord Jesus, receive my spirit." Then he fell on his knees and cried out, "Lord, do not hold this sin against them." When he had said this, he fell asleep."

—Acts 7:52b-60 (NIV)

D$_{ID}$ you hear and feel Stephen's passion and conviction in these verses? Did you see his servant's heart? God gave Stephen a revelation while the people were stoning him. Stephen saw Jesus, the Son of Man, standing. The Bible says Jesus is seated at the right hand of God, but in this instance, He was standing because He saw a man after His own heart. When Stephen forgave the ones stoning him, he received a revelation of Jesus as the Son of Man, our Redeemer. Jesus was the only one who ever referred to Himself as the Son of Man, meaning he was both divine and human. Both natures were embodied in Him. Mark 2:10 tells us only the Son of Man had the power to forgive sins, and as our Redeemer, Jesus forgives sins.

I$_{N}$ $_{THE}$ O$_{LD}$ T$_{ESTAMENT}$, Jesus is a type of Kinsman Redeemer. A Kinsman Redeemer was a blood relative who would pay the price to rescue and redeem family members from hardship. In some cases, as seen in the Book of Ruth, this person would marry the deceased relative's widow to preserve the family name and leave them a legacy.

Jesus referred to Himself as the Son of Man because He had to be human to shed His blood and relate us to God. Only in His human nature and not in His divine nature could His blood be shed to forgive sins. Jesus came as our Kinsman Redeemer to pay the price and relate us to God because He is our blood relative, our elder brother. Stephen was given this inside revelation of who Jesus is as he lay dying for the cause of Christ. Stephen saw Jesus—usually seated next to the

Father—standing because Jesus was witnessing the death of a man with the heart of a servant. A heart like His.

As STEPHEN DIED, he demonstrated how truly like Christ his heart was. He forgave those who were stoning him, as Jesus forgave those who nailed Him to the cross of Calvary. Stephen was connected to the nature of God.

For you and me to have a heart like Stephen, the heart of a servant, we must give ourselves totally over to God. Understand your history with God and know He will do for you all He did for those men and women in the Bible. Let the world know you cannot accomplish anything without God's help. Show them how dependent you are on His grace and mercy by allowing Him to step into your difficult situations and wrap His arms of love, mercy, and grace around you to bring healing in the difficulties. Be determined and steadfast when you embrace God's plans for your life. Set your face like flint as you race toward your destiny. Don't stumble into your destiny by accident; pursue God so He can reveal it to you, and you can embrace all of it when He does.

WHEN YOU PUT your hands on the plow, go with God. Do not look backward. Do not take your eyes off Jesus because all God has for you is in front and not behind you. He said to forget those things which are behind and reach for those things before you press toward the mark for the prize of the high calling of God in Christ Jesus (Philippians 3:13).

As YOU DEVELOP the heart of a servant, you will begin to look like Christ and will readily forgive people when they hurt or disappoint you. Like Stephen, do everything you can so you will not miss the joy of knowing one day, Jesus will stand up from His throne to cheer you on as He welcomes you home. I can hear Him saying to you, "Job well done. Job well done. Now, enter into the joy of the Lord!"

CHAPTER 4
A COMMITTED HEART

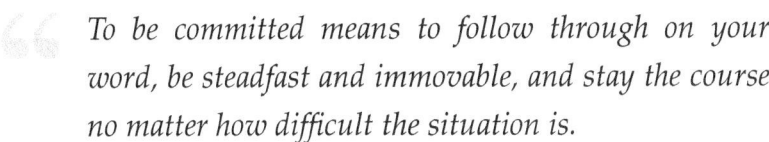

To be committed means to follow through on your word, be steadfast and immovable, and stay the course no matter how difficult the situation is.

In chapter three, we talked about the life of Stephen. While committed to Christ, Stephen demonstrated what a heart of commitment looks like. In this chapter, you come to a deeper understanding of what it means to have a heart overflowing with commitment and reap the benefits of staying committed.

Commitment is defined as a pledge or a word given to someone that is as binding as a contract. To be committed means to follow through on your word, be steadfast and immovable, and stay the course no matter how difficult the situation is. As we examine our lives and connection to God, we must ask ourselves some questions.

HAVE I BEEN A COMMITTED PERSON? Has my heart remained steadfast in the things I have committed to do? Has commitment been the cornerstone of my life? Is my heart so committed that, like Stephen, I would give my life for the cause of Christ? As you meditate on these questions, you will discover what you are most committed to and how passionate you are in following through on your word. You will also understand where your heart is concerning God and His plans for you.

THE STORY of Ruth paints a beautiful picture of a heart that was entirely committed to her mother-in-law, Naomi. She was so committed that she walked away from her people, her country, and her idol gods to follow the widow into her life, world, and difficult situations. Ruth's commitment to Naomi gives us an example of the level of commitment you and I should have toward God. Her dedication was genuine and sure, and nothing moved her away from keeping her promise and staying the course as she journeyed home with Naomi. We must be so entirely committed to our relationship with God that nothing, and no one, can move us away from Him.

True Commitment

But Ruth replied, "Don't ask me to leave you and turn back. Wherever you go, I will go; wherever you live, I will live. Your people will be my people, and your God will be my God. Wherever you die, I will die, and there I will be buried. May the LORD punish me severely if I allow anything but death to separate us!"

When Naomi saw that Ruth was determined to go with her, she said nothing more. So the two of them continued on their journey. When they came to Bethlehem, the entire town was excited by their arrival. "Is it really Naomi?" the women asked. "Don't call me Naomi," she responded. "Instead, call me Mara, for the Almighty has made my life very bitter for me. I went away full, but the LORD has brought me home empty. Why call me Naomi when the LORD has caused me to suffer and the Almighty has sent such tragedy upon me?"
—Ruth 1:16-21 (NLT)

THE STORY of Ruth and Naomi is one of genuine commitment. Naomi's name means "Pleasant one," and Ruth's means "Friendship." Ruth demonstrated her friendship with Naomi by laying down her life for her friend and mother-in-law. Ruth was a Moabite woman who married one of Naomi's sons after they went to live in the land of Moab because of the famine in Bethlehem. When Naomi's husband and sons died, leaving her without any means of support, this precipitated her return to her homeland with hopes that a close relative would provide for her. Ruth chose to leave her old life, family, and friends and make the journey with Naomi because she was dedicated to Naomi, who needed her love and care. Through this simple act of love, she took a massive leap of faith, venturing into a strange land. Ruth's commitment to Naomi caused her to receive a reward for her loyalty, and it also transformed Naomi's life.

IN THE ABOVE SCRIPTURE, Naomi wanted to change her name to Mara, which means bitterness, because she felt God had abandoned her with the death of all the men in her family. Naomi thought God was punishing her because she and her family left Him when they went to live in Moab. But, regardless of how Naomi felt, God had not abandoned her. Instead, He had positioned Ruth in her life as His blessing to her.

Even though Ruth did not know what she would encounter, her determination to journey home with her mother-in-law displayed a depth of love and commitment to Naomi that could only have been sent to her by God. This commitment nourished Naomi's soul, for she realized Ruth cared enough to follow her into an uncertain future. Naomi's walk with the Lord was influenced because God had put someone in her life who would become as dear to her as a son.

THE LEVEL of Ruth's commitment caused Naomi to reconnect to God and gave her comfort on the arduous journey and even into old age. Ruth's unconditional commitment displayed God's unconditional love and devotion to Naomi. Naomi realized since Ruth did not abandon her in her need, God also had not abandoned her during her crisis. Ruth's commitment helped Naomi regain a sense of fullness in her life. Naomi discovered that while she was planning to live a life filled with bitterness, God was preparing a life that would abound with new blessings. Since Naomi was too old to remarry and have additional sons, God made provision through Ruth's marriage to one of Naomi's relatives.

IT WAS NOT an accident that Naomi's son married Ruth instead of another woman in her country. God knew Ruth's heart and character even though she served pagan gods, and He knew Ruth would turn her heart over to Him and allow Him to use her as He intended. God had prepared for Naomi, a daughter-in-law whose commitment to her reflected God's commitment to her. He gave Naomi a daughter willing to lay her own life down to preserve her mother-in-law's life.

GOD HAD A DESTINY FOR RUTH, and her purpose brought a new direction to Naomi's life. Even though Naomi thought God had abandoned her and He had no further use for her, God brought her into a new season. This season was filled with blessings and rewards unlike any she had experienced. God did not leave Naomi, even though she and her family had left Him for a while. God was always with Naomi. He provided her with a daughter who was totally committed to her and faithfully provided for her needs.

ROMANS 8:38-39 demonstrates the level of God's commitment to us.

I am convinced that nothing can separate us from God's love. Neither death nor life, neither angels nor demons, neither our fears for today nor our worries about tomorrow - not even the powers of hell can separate us from God's love. No power in the sky above or in the earth below - indeed, nothing in all creation will ever be able to separate us from the love of God that is revealed in Christ Jesus our Lord.

THIS IS GOD'S extraordinary commitment to each of His children. His commitment caused Him to give His Son's life for us. Jesus' commitment to God and us drove Him to lay down His life to redeem us. Our commitment will allow us to lay down our lives for Him and others.

COMMITMENT HELPS US hold tightly to what has been entrusted to us. It keeps us pressing into the purposes of God and His promise of eternal life. God's commitment to us, as seen in Romans 8, should spark a response from us. Our response should be a heart that is entirely devoted and committed to Him. Are you convinced that nothing would change God's love, devotion, or commitment to you? The more convinced you are of this, the more you will stay committed and connected to Him.

GOD WAS with Naomi in a foreign country, on her return journey home, when she had no provider, and in the darkest moments of her life. Because of her losses, Naomi felt God was punishing her; instead, He was preparing a bright future for her. He was working on a new beginning and preparing to bring abundant favor to her life. God is doing the same thing on your behalf. He will never forget your labor of love for Him, even when you stray at times.

Commitment Contains Power

God first teaches us commitment by demonstrating His faithfulness to us. He is always with us no matter where we are in our relationship with Him. God released His power, the Holy Spirit, into our lives when we committed to serving and following Jesus Christ. He gives us the strength to live a life that is pleasing to Him.

- GOD GIVES us the power to glorify His Son
- To step away from hopelessness and live in hope
- Triumph during difficulties
- Live lives crowned with integrity
- Live a life of morality
- Be victorious in the seasons of crisis
- To commit to others who are in need
- Follow through on our word
- Stay the course even when life becomes difficult

GOD'S POWER is released in His commitment to fulfill every promise He has given us in His Word. As we take His Word and live by it, power is released into our hearts, giving us victory over every work of the evil one. God's Word is filled with power, and His Word is a compass that will guide us through the storms of life. God's Word teaches us how to walk by faith, live in faith, and be committed no matter the season of our life.

RUTH DISCOVERED the power of commitment. Her commitment to Naomi not only gained her a godly husband but also put her in the lineage of Jesus Christ. Her commitment altered the course of her life; it brought her into the amazing destiny God had planned for her. Ruth's commitment to God and Naomi gave Naomi a new purpose in her old age. Like Ruth, Stephen's commitment to God caused him to receive great rewards when he met the Lord face-to-face. Like their commitment, our commitment to God and others will forever change the course of our destiny and our direction, purpose, and goals.

As you look closely at your heart, how committed are you to God? Understand that reconnecting to God more profoundly requires you to commit to Him—His ways, His plans, and His purposes for your life. Reconnect today and experience the blessings that come from being committed!

CHAPTER 5
A DEDICATED HEART

Some of us have lost our intimate connection to God. As a result, we are not experiencing the blessings, favor, provision, and fullness of life He intends us to have.

To reconnect our hearts to God, we must rededicate our lives to Him, so He can saturate us with the wellspring of living water that flows from His heart toward us. Dedication means to be devoted to the one you love. It is to consecrate yourself, to give all you have to the source of your commitment, to be honorable in your intentions, to be considerate, and to show favor. Our devotion must first be toward God because He has demonstrated His complete devotion toward us.

Devotion

*My old self has been crucified with Christ. It is no longer I who live,
but Christ lives in me. So I live in this earthly body by trusting in
the Son of God, who loved me and gave himself for me.*
—Galatians 2:20 (NLT)

OUR FIRST ACT of devotion is to move out of the way so God
can be enthroned in our hearts. We must acknowledge there
is One who is more significant than us, and He must take
center stage in our lives. Devotion is how we allow God to be
the only One to live and reign entirely in our hearts and lives.
His great love for us motivates us to serve Him and fulfill His
plans on earth.

The Scripture above tells us when Jesus was crucified, we
were crucified along with Him. As a result, we no longer live,
but He is daily living through us. We were a part of Jesus
when He took the beatings, bled, and died on the Cross.

Jesus died for our sins and to free us from shame. In being
crucified with Him, we have died to our plans, old lifestyles,
will, and desire to have things our way. We are now dedicated to what He wants to accomplish through us. Our dedication to Him means we have taken on His plans, will, ways,
and desires.

TO BE DEVOTED ALSO MEANS you have the attitude and willingness to give and to lay down your life for the Savior. This
was Stephen's attitude and heart. His love for the Savior was
so intense he allowed himself to be stoned to death and did

not run away from those holding the stones. While dying, there was only one name on Stephen's lips—the name of his beloved Jesus. Stephen was boldly declaring the price Jesus paid to ransom and redeem mankind. He was so devoted and dedicated to Christ that even as he took his last breath, he asked God to forgive those who were stoning him.

OUR DEVOTION MUST BE intense enough for us to lay down our lives. We must willingly lay down all the weights and sins that so quickly overtake us and press toward Jesus Christ because of the exorbitant price He paid to reunite us with our Father. Our devotion to Him will cause us to give our lives away daily, so we can point lost humanity to Him. We show dedication in our commitment, actions, attitudes, and everyday choices. Our devotion should say, "We will do nothing to bring shame, hurt, or embarrassment to the One we love." When we stay true to our commitments, act in accordance with His will, maintain a positive attitude, and then make choices that glorify God, we display our sincere dedication and devotion to Him.

A Heart to Give

ONCE YOU become dedicated and devoted to the Lord, you will discover you have been equipped with a heart that desires to give. Dedication requires you to give of yourself to others. In giving, you demonstrate that you are created in the image of the Father, Son, and Holy Spirit because they always give to us. The Father hears and answers us when we pray;

the Son shows us compassion and love when we slip and fall from grace, and the Holy Spirit comforts and leads us away from evil and onto paths that honor the Son. Let us look at a passage in Luke 6 to see what happens when you and I have the heart to give.

Give, and you will receive. Your gift will return to you in full - pressed down, shaken together to make room for more, running over, and poured into your lap. The amount you give will determine the amount you get back.
—Luke 6:38 (NLT)

GOD USES our giving to bless and prosper us. We have many things to offer besides money, like our time, love, support, and prayers. The promise in the scripture is whatever you give will be given back to you, and it will be returned in a more significant measure. You release what you have, and then God multiplies it back to you.

The Scripture says when God gives back to you, He presses it down and shakes it up. Why? When something is pressed down and shaken, it settles and makes room in the container for more. Therefore, whatever you give from your heart to God and others, God takes and presses it down, shakes it up, and then He goes a step further and causes it to run over into your life. The blessings God returns to you will run over because there will not be room enough to handle the abundant supply God will keep pouring out.

SOME OF US may attempt to receive the Lord's blessings in our hands, but because He always goes above and beyond what we can think or imagine, He must pour His blessings into our laps. Our hands are not large enough to contain His tremendous supply. God intends for you to overflow so that your life (present and future) cannot hold the favor, blessings, provisions, and fullness of joy He has in store for you. He will cause men, women, boys, and girls —people everywhere—to give into your life. When you are devoted to God and have the heart to give out what He has given to you, God will make sure that what you receive in return is far greater than what you gave away.

GIVING REQUIRES SACRIFICE. During one of my seasons of unemployment, the Lord asked me to take three hundred dollars from my savings. Since my mortgage payment was coming due, I naturally assumed He was giving me instructions about what I needed to do to pay the bill. Later that week, I went to my Home Group Bible Study. During the session, we prayed over the needs of the people. One couple shared they were about to lose their home because they could not pay their mortgage. You guessed it! God did not tell me to withdraw the three hundred dollars for my mortgage but for theirs.

When God instructed me to give the money to the couple, I had an intense conversation with Him. Our conversation started with something like this, "God, are You truly asking me to plant this seed into them when my mortgage is due, and I don't even have the full amount to pay it?" His response was a resounding "Yes." I continued with my discourse about how I had been unemployed for months, how no opportunity had yet come through, and I did not know when a job would be forthcoming. He did not respond throughout this dialogue because He was waiting on my obedience to His instructions. After a long pause, I finally obeyed and asked Him to give me joy as I gave the money to meet the couple's needs. The couple received the money, thankfully, and prayed for blessings to return to me.

God later paid my mortgage and took it a step further. During my one year of unemployment, I was never late paying a bill or short on any payments. In this situation, I learned to have the heart to give to others in need.

I am required to give when things are going well in my life when I have extra money, and when I am in need. As I share during my time of need, I demonstrate my trust and confidence in God's ability to provide for me. This principle applies to giving money and all areas of life. As we learn to give our lives away to help others, God will abundantly supply what we need. Remember, God is a rewarder, and He will reward you for everything you give in His name and for His glory.

To Be Honorable

DEDICATION AND HONOR go hand in hand; both speak of the intentions of our hearts. Honor means to be full of integrity, to be respectful, and to be respected. To be honorable, we must first understand to whom honor is due. All honor belongs to God!

THEN DAVID PRAISED the LORD in the presence of the whole

assembly: "O LORD, the God of our ancestor Israel, may you be
praised forever and ever! Yours, O LORD, is the greatness, the
power, the glory, the victory, and the majesty. Everything in the
heavens and on earth is yours, O LORD, and this is your kingdom.
We adore you as the one who is over all things. Wealth and honor
come from you alone, for you rule over everything. Power and
might are in your hand, and at your discretion, people are made
great and give strength. O our God, we thank you and praise your
glorious name!"
—1 Chronicles 29:10-13 (NLT)

THE HONOR is due to God because He is El Elyon, the Most
High God. Everything in heaven and earth is under His absolute control, and He displays His splendor in everything we
see. As His children, we must glorify Him regularly because
He is worthy of all honor and praise. Our lives, intentions,
and motives must always be honorable. The Holy Spirit's
power in our hearts enables us to be honorable in our dealings with God and people, and He causes us to make decisions that honor God. The power of the Holy Spirit living in
Stephen's heart made him honorable. Stephen would not
back down from confronting the Jews or showing them how
willing and determined they were to kill Jesus.

WHEN THE DISCIPLES initially selected Stephen as one of
their leaders, they recognized he was full of honor and
integrity. They saw a man who had the heart to honor and
revere God. For you and me to live honorably, God must
dominate our lives. We must allow Him to rule and guide us
each step of the way. Daily, we must choose to do what is

right and honorable in His sight. Sometimes our choice to be honorable may lead us down difficult paths because we decide to do what is right. Like Stephen, we must choose to walk this difficult road, which so few people travel, so that we may be a true reflection of Christ for those seeking a relationship with Him. Stephen held tightly to his honor even as he faced death.

Examine your heart closely. Is it filled with honor? Are you walking and serving with integrity? The answers to these questions will help you see how closely you resemble Christ and how well you honor Him for all the great things He has done for you.

To Be Considerate

CONSIDERATION REQUIRES a deliberate act from each of us. When we are considerate of others, we seek to be a blessing to them. Consideration and dedication will produce a harvest in our lives and the lives of those needing a helping hand. To be considerate means we say yes whenever a need is presented to us, and we can fulfill it. Consideration begins in our hearts because it is from our hearts we esteem others highly and decide to provide for their needs. Not only do we need to be considerate toward people, but we must show consideration to God. The following passage of scripture tells us what happens when we do not consider God.

THEN THE LORD sent this message through the prophet Haggai: "Why are you living in luxurious houses while my house lies in

ruins?" This is what the LORD of Heaven's Armies says: Look at what's happening to you! You have planted much but harvest little. You eat but are not satisfied. You drink but are still thirsty. You put on clothes but cannot keep warm. Your wages disappear as though you were putting them in pockets filled with holes! This is what the LORD of Heaven's Armies says: Look at what's happening to you! Now go up into the hills, bring down timber, and rebuild my house. Then I will take pleasure in it and be honored, says the LORD.
—Haggai 1:3-8 (NLT)

In this Scripture, God questioned the people because they lacked consideration for and dedication to the things that concerned Him. He asked why they had not paid attention to His house (the Sanctuary), which was in ruins. Instead, they were steadily building grand houses for themselves.

He challenged them to consider their motives and whether life was more about pleasing themselves than pleasing Him. He told them that when they took care of their needs first, instead of considering what He needed, they would always come up short. Their needs were unmet because they lacked the consideration required to have a proper relationship with Him.

God used their everyday struggles to make them see they were in error. He told them their hard work would not produce a harvest in their lives; it is the blessing of the Lord that makes us rich. The people ate and drank but were still hungry because there was an emptiness in their hearts and souls. The people remained hungry because they did not consider God's needs. They could not keep warm even when dressed in warm clothing because they were not in alignment with His will for their lives. They worked, toiled, and labored, but their money seeped out of their hands because God was not acknowledged as their provider. Since the people were not caring for God's House, God was not taking care of their needs.

Does this sound familiar to anyone? You have done all you can but cannot seem to get a breakthrough. You pray, work, and toil long and hard, but nothing works for you. Here is God's answer: Give careful thought to your ways! Are you listening to God's instructions for your life and what He wants you to do with your resources? Is it the desire of your heart to please Him? Do you see others in need yet pass them by even though you have the means to bless them?

Are you obedient to God's voice? If your deepest desire is to please God, first take care of what He has asked you to do and do it without delay. When you obey God and consider His needs, God will feed, clothe, dress, and keep you warm. He will meet your financial, emotional, spiritual, and relational needs.

We must understand that God comes first and consider what matters to Him. Look closely at yourself and consider your actions, so you will not be led astray. Consider your attitude so that you will give with a cheerful heart. The thoughtfulness, kindness, and compassion we extend when we are considerate and help meet others' needs demonstrate the love of God. Let us consider our ways and make them pleasing to God. Then, He will give us success in whatever we are doing.

. . .

Showing and Receiving Favor

BEFORE WE CONCLUDE this chapter on dedication, let us look at one more thing that will cause us to be dedicated to God. To experience His favor, we must first acknowledge God wants to pour His abundant favor and blessings on us. To walk in favor, we must take an interest in God and in the things that interest Him. As God shows us favor, we must also show favor to others.

A GOOD MAN SHOWETH FAVOR, and lendeth: he will guide his affairs with discretion. Surely he shall not be moved forever: the righteous shall be in everlasting remembrance. He shall not be afraid of evil tidings: his heart is fixed, trusting the LORD.
His heart is established, he shall not be afraid, until he sees his desire upon his enemies. He hath dispersed, he hath given to the poor; his righteousness endureth forever; his horn shall be exalted with honor.
—Psalm 112:5-9 (KJV)

THE FIRST THING we see in this Scripture is when we show favor to others, God gives us justice in our affairs. He tells us people who operate in favor will never be shaken because of bad news, nor will they be disillusioned. Favor enriches our lives because our hearts are confident and secure in the Lord. It increases our lives and allows us to give to the poor. When we give to the poor, the Bible promises our righteousness will endure forever. Favor brings us honor and causes us to be promoted. We have victory in all circumstances and over the enemy when favored. As you show favor to others, God will ensure you are highly favored. When you show favor:

- It brings a shield of protection to your life.
- Opens doors for you and gives you preferential treatment.
- It brings promotion and increases to your life, even ahead of people who are more qualified than you are.
- It will cause breakthroughs in your life.
- It will bring you an abundance of good things, which will cause you to increase so that you can be a more incredible blessing in the Kingdom of God.

WHEN YOU ARE DEDICATED to the Lord, He enriches your life with beautiful blessings and places His hand of favor on you so that you will prosper and succeed. Dedication means you desire to stay in the center of God's will. It means you will remain close to Him so you can hear adequately, see clearly, and understand you can do all things through Christ who strengthens you (Philippians 4:13).

As you look at people around you and see God's favor in their lives, remember, that you can receive and serve in God's continual favor as well. He has blessed you because He loves you and desires to see you live a joyful life. Your willingness to adhere to all the things God has asked you to do shows him your dedication.

Do you desire God's favor in your life? If your answer is "Yes," then your dedication to Him will produce the blessing of God in your midst and give you victory over every circumstance you face. Declare this with me, "I will walk and live in God's abundant favor each day of my life."

CHAPTER 6
A TRUSTWORTHY HEART

Trust is a crucial factor in our relationships not only with God but with others as well. Trust is the cornerstone for building a lasting, durable connection.

Without trust, we will never be delighted with the outcome of our life. Trust is the glue that holds us together. Trust speaks of being dependable, reliable, faithful, believable, credible, and loyal. A person with a trustworthy heart is dependable; you can count on them. Are you one of these people? When others think about you, do they naturally think of how reliable you are and that you can be counted on whether things are going well or there is a crisis?

A TRUSTWORTHY PERSON understands as they trust God with all their heart, He will pour His goodness and blessings into their lives. This person has learned they must lean on

God and not on their understanding of how things should be. They understand God must be consulted in every decision, and they depend on Him and obey His instructions. God has become the center, the focus of their life. When God is the center of your life, you will consult Him in every decision because you understand He can be trusted to lead you down paths that will bring blessings and honor to Him.

Since our understanding of things is often limited, we must find wisdom and answers in God's Word. When we seek God for wisdom and insight, we trust in Him. When we remember God is a good God; that He is faithful and cannot lie; and that He is always with us and promised to take care of us; then we can relax in our relationship with Him because we are assured He can be trusted and has the very best in store for us.

MANY START TRUSTING and being faithful to God, but not everyone finishes well. On our journey, we sometimes miss significant crossroads that God shows us or take the wrong path and get totally off course. There are many examples of this in the Word of God, and they are given to help guide us so we stay faithful to Him and connected to His heart.

Look with me at King Hezekiah's story because it shows how we can be doing great one moment, and the next moment, we can veer from God's way and onto the wrong path. "Hezekiah was twenty-five years old when he became the king of Judah, and he reigned in Jerusalem for twenty-nine years. He did what was pleasing in the LORD'S sight, just as his ancestor David had done" 2 Chronicles 29:1-2 (NLT).

HEZEKIAH'S LIFE STARTED WELL, but as you read his story, he did not finish well. He began his life being trustworthy and faithful, but something caused him to detour from this path. May his story prompt you to check where you are in your relationship with God and allow you to see how closely connected you are to His heart.

HEZEKIAH'S NAME means "God is my strength." The first thing we read about him is he pleased the Lord. How? He did what was right in the sight of the Lord. He modeled the example of David, a man after God's heart. He prayed and sought the Lord when he needed wisdom, answers, and directions. Hezekiah sought God's help when the Assyrian army came against him, and God delivered him. He was devoted to God and trusted Him without reservation. Hezekiah focused his heart entirely on worshiping the Lord and brought the art of worship back to the temple of God.

THE PREVIOUS KING had turned his back on God and led God's people astray. This king took all the articles from God's temple, broke them into pieces, and then shut the temple doors so no one could worship God there. He then set up pagan altars on every corner of Jerusalem so the people could worship. He walked away from God and took others with him.

HEZEKIAH'S first act of devotion was to restore worship to the house of God. He called the people to a seven-day worship festival, which lasted another seven days because God showed up in such great power. When the people took the time to worship Him, God came down and blessed them and their land. He caused their fields to produce tremendous harvests and their animals to reproduce abundantly, so the people gave a tithe of all their blessing. Their harvest was so abundant it took them beyond late spring and into autumn to gather all God had given them.

ALTHOUGH HEZEKIAH was initially trustworthy, faithful, and dependable, he got off track. As seen in the Scripture below, he strayed off course when he faced his first major test and missed a significant time honoring God with his life. Like Hezekiah, we can start exceptionally well but also get off course; therefore, we must guard our hearts and check our motives, so pride and self-indulgence do not get in.

ABOUT THAT TIME HEZEKIAH became deathly ill. He prayed to the LORD, who healed him and gave him a miraculous sign. But Hezekiah did not respond appropriately to the kindness shown him, and he became proud. So the LORD'S anger came against him and against Judah and Jerusalem. Then Hezekiah humbled himself and repented of his pride, as did the people of Jerusalem. So the LORD'S anger did not fall on them during Hezekiah's lifetime. However, when ambassadors arrived from Babylon to ask about the remarkable events that had taken place in the land, God withdrew from Hezekiah in order to test him and to see what was really in his heart.
—2 Chronicles 32:24-26; 31 (NLT)

HEZEKIAH'S FAITHFULNESS to God and trustworthiness were tested when sickness attacked his body. After God healed him, he became prideful about his acquisitions from the Lord and was no longer thankful for all God had done for him.

God had given Hezekiah immense wealth, and he had to build buildings to hold all the silver, gold, precious stones, spices, shields, and many other unique gifts God had caused him to receive. Hezekiah also built storehouses to store the grains, olive oil, and wine God gave him.

In addition, as God continued to bless him, he constructed many stalls to house his cattle, sheep, goats, flocks, and herds. Hezekiah's wealth was so abundant other towns had to be built to store it. God was tremendously faithful to Hezekiah because he had been trustworthy in his initial service to God. God decided to withdraw His protection from Hezekiah for a season to see how trustworthy, dependable, reliable, and loyal Hezekiah's heart still was toward Him. We must continuously examine our hearts because God is watching to see if we, too, will become proud and walk away from serving Him after He has blessed us.

GOD'S response to Hezekiah's sickness shows His compassion for His children.

ABOUT THAT TIME Hezekiah became deathly ill, and the prophet Isaiah son of Amoz went to visit him. He gave the king this message: "This is what the LORD says: Set your affairs in order, for you are going to die. You will not recover from this illness." When Hezekiah heard this, he turned his face to the wall and prayed to the LORD, "Remember, O LORD, how I have always been faithful to you and have served you single-mindedly, always doing what pleases you." Then he broke down and wept bitterly. But before Isaiah had left the middle courtyard, this message came to him from the LORD. "Go back to Hezekiah, the leader of my people. Tell him,

'This is what the LORD, the God of your ancestor David, says: I
have heard your prayer and seen your tears. I will heal you, and
three days from now you will get out of bed and go to the Temple of
the Lord. I will add fifteen years to your life, and I will rescue you
and this city from the king of Assyria. I will defend this city for my
own honor and for the sake of my servant David."
—2 Kings 20:1-6 (NLT)

LET me begin by encouraging you to read the entire chapter to see how faithful God was to Hezekiah and how Hezekiah missed this divine opportunity to glorify God. You do not want to miss your divine opportunity to give glory to God. The first thing we see in this Scripture is after Hezekiah became sick, the prophet Isaiah went to visit him, carrying a strong message from the Lord. Isaiah said, "Hezekiah, you are going to die!" How devastating the news must have been to Hezekiah since he knew this word was from God. The prophet Isaiah was known as a prophet who delivered accurate words from the Lord. Isaiah told him to get his house and his affairs in order. Did you notice Hezekiah was blessed by the Lord and had an intimate relationship with God, yet his house was not in order?

WE ARE OFTEN busy in our service to God, yet our lives are out of order. If our lives are not in order, we do not reflect the level of excellence that allows us to represent God well to others. God wanted Hezekiah's affairs for his successor. Why did God allow the sickness, and why was the prophet Isaiah's message so intense and piercing? This difficult season in Hezekiah's life would test his character, faithfulness, devotion, and trustworthiness to God. Isaiah's message was solid and piercing because Hezekiah had become complacent in his relationship with God and needed to be shaken.

HEZEKIAH DID what most of us do when faced with bad news. He prayed, cried, and begged God for His help and deliverance. Hezekiah boldly reminded God how he had faithfully walked before Him, was wholehearted in his service, and did things that pleased Him. God not only heard him but also remembered and responded to his cry for help. Before Isaiah could leave the courtyard, God sent him back to Hezekiah with a new message. God had heard Hezekiah's prayer, seen his tears, and would give him fifteen more years of life.

As WE LOOK CLOSELY at Hezekiah's response, we will see how the enemy can keep us from receiving all the blessings the Lord has in store for us. When Isaiah told Hezekiah he would die, he *instantly* believed the report. However, when Isaiah went back and told him God was going to heal him and give him fifteen more years, Hezekiah did not *instantly* believe the word. Instead, he asked for a sign. He did not receive and accept the report about being healed but had readily received the information about his death.

WE MUST PAUSE HERE for a moment and think back on how many bad reports we have also received and believed, yet we struggle to hear and apply the truth God is speaking to us. Our lack of trust in God's Word can affect our lives and relationships with Him. Hezekiah questioned the word God had sent him through the prophet. God gave him a sign, but his doubt demonstrated a lack of trust. Hezekiah had gone from being trustworthy to one who no longer believed in the Word of God. God healed Hezekiah, but his life spiraled out of control. Hezekiah became proud and arrogant. He stopped trusting God and no longer sought His wisdom but did what seemed right in his own eyes.

ONE DAY, the king of Babylon sent Hezekiah gifts and well wishes, which he readily accepted without consulting the Lord. He showed the king's messengers everything in his palace—all the treasures God had given him— without considering their motives toward him might not be pure. Hezekiah had an opportunity to tell the messengers about his God, who God was, how God had healed him, and that God was his salvation, but he did not. Hezekiah did not introduce the messengers to the One who had abundantly blessed him. He forgot his God! He quickly showed them all the wonderful things God had given him but failed to mention God. We cannot judge him too fast or too harshly since some of us may be guilty of the same thing.

THE PROPHET ISAIAH came back with another word for Hezekiah. He asked who the strangers were and what they had seen in his palace. Hezekiah told him he had shown them everything. God's final message to Hezekiah was the Babylonians would take everything in his court, including the treasures he had acquired and those he had received from his ancestors. They would also take all his sons, and they would become slaves to the Babylonian king. Hezekiah responded, "This message you have given me from the Lord is good."

How could this message be construed as good? He showed no concern upon hearing that a heathen group of people would take God's blessings and treasures from him, his sons would become slaves, and he would lose all his ancestral gifts. Hezekiah was no longer trustworthy. He had become selfish and self-absorbed, caring only about his well-being. The Bible tells us what Hezekiah thought when Isaiah gave him the word, "At least there will be peace and security during my lifetime" (2 Kings 20:15-19).

HEZEKIAH STARTED out being faithful and trustworthy, but wealth and the many blessings God had given him, which should have caused him to be thankful, and to glorify God, filled him with pride and caused him to stray from God's protection. Hezekiah was blessed and influential initially, but he ended with a diminished life and a poor testimony. Hezekiah chose to be no longer trustworthy, and he stopped being faithful to God.

WHERE ARE you on your walk? How will your story end? You can remain trustworthy to God and have a strong finish.

Faithfulness

If you are faithful in little things, you will be faithful in large ones. But if you are dishonest in little things, you won't be honest with greater responsibilities.
—Luke 16:10 (NLT)

FAITHFULNESS IS a key to trustworthiness. To be faithful, you must be filled with faith. Meaning you have faith in God and His plans and promises for you. Faithfulness is measured by your willingness to handle the little things in your life as they are most important. This means you consider the small things and don't neglect them, even if they seem insignificant. For example, God may have called you to lead a group of uncommitted people. Even though the attendance may be small, God still expects you to be timely, consistent, and committed to meeting with them. Your commitment and faithfulness will later promote you to more significant opportunities. We often want to bypass the mundane to get to what we think is more exciting. Some people look at numbers and think God is more involved in everything that is large and on a grand scale. However, God's presence can be found in more minor activities as much as it can be found in larger ones.

THE SCRIPTURES POINT us to the fact that God will only entrust Kingdom blessings, favor, and greatness to those who are faithful, trustworthy, honest, and filled with integrity. Demonstrating faithfulness means you talk about it and live it out daily. Stephen was filled with faith and faithful in his service to God. Understand that God expects you to be faithful to whatever has been assigned.

OVER THE YEARS, I have volunteered in several churches and a few organizations, and I have discovered that far too few people genuinely understand what it means to be faithful. Fortunately, I have worked with some whose faithfulness is top-notch; they always go above and beyond the call of duty. These people not only do what they promise to do and what is expected, but they consistently exceed expectations. They are trustworthy, faithful, dependable, and can be counted on to be where they are assigned and do what has been assigned to them. They genuinely understand they are serving the Lord. They realize they are not serving a church, organization, or leaders but God. They work as unto Him without withholding any part of themselves.

In our ministry, I have seen this dedication and faithful service inspiring me to do more for God. As you look at the tapestry of faithful people's lives, you see their deep commitment to God. Because He has first place in their hearts, they give freely of themselves in service to Him and others. These people know their God, and because He has been so faithful to them, they have decided to spend their lives serving Him. This does not mean God has given them everything they requested. The opposite is true in most cases, yet, they remain steadfast and faithful.

Your assignments test your level of faithfulness. God watches over you to see if you will pass the test of being faithful in the small tasks then He can promote you to bigger and greater things. On a scale of one to ten, with ten being the highest, how faithful are you in your commitment, your Christian walk, your relationship with God, and your relationships with others?

Believable

Believability goes along with faithfulness. As seen in Acts 7, Stephen was a man who served God with all he had, and he believed in the Word of God. Before Stephen was stoned to death, he told the Israeli people who Jesus was and how He had fulfilled five hundred prophesies spoken about Him before His birth, beginning in the book of

Genesis and going all the way through to the New Testament.

Stephen was so believable his words pierced the hearts of the Jews to the point they covered their ears and ground their teeth together in frustration. With the Holy Spirit's power, Stephen reminded them they had killed the one true Son of the living God because they would not let go of their religious beliefs. He was believable because He knew God, loved His Son and was willing to give His life to make Jesus known to those who rejected Him.

TO BE BELIEVABLE, you must be a committed believer and be able to persuade others to your way of thinking. You must have total conviction about your beliefs and sell them your ideas. Your assurance and certainty about what you believe make you credible. Stephen demonstrated all these traits and brought intense conviction to the hearts of the Jews by sharing the Word of God with them. For you and me to attain this level of believability, we must be filled with God's wisdom and knowledge. Paul tells us how to gain wisdom and knowledge.

EVER SINCE I first heard of your strong faith in the Lord Jesus and your love for God's people everywhere, I have not stopped thanking God for you. I pray for you constantly, asking God, the glorious Father of our Lord Jesus Christ, to give you spiritual wisdom and insight so that you might grow in your knowledge of God. I pray that you hearts will be flooded with light so that you can understand the confident hope he has given to those he called - his holy people who are his rich and glorious inheritance. I also pray

that you will understand the incredible greatness of God's power for
us who believe him.
—Ephesians 1:15-19 (NLT)

The Apostle Paul was writing to the people of Ephesus, faithful followers of the Lord Jesus. He desired to bless and encourage them for their dedication and commitment to the cause of Christ. Paul wanted the believers to experience all the richness that could be found in a deep and intimate relationship with Christ, so he earnestly prayed for them. Paul understood for these believers to attain all God had for them and enjoy the riches of Kingdom life, they had to be filled with the wisdom of God. Believers must be filled with the wisdom and revelation of God, so they can share His insight with others and draw them into a deeper relationship with Him.

PAUL ASKED GOD to flood the believers' hearts with light. To be inundated with the light of God's Holy Spirit would cause them to see more clearly. He asked God to pull back the curtain and unveil the hidden things in their hearts. God was to give them unique insight that could only be obtained through Him. He would show them what was about to unfold in their midst. As God opened their eyes and unveiled their hearts, enlightenment would come, and His ideas and plans would be revealed to them. With this enlightenment, the wisdom of God would penetrate their hearts, and they would receive, begin to experience His riches, enjoy their inheritance, and tap into the power available to them.

THIS PRAYER IS also for you and me! God wants us to be

believable so we can speak for Him. He wants our vision to be clear to warn us of impending danger or great opportunities. God wants us to see and hear clearly, so we can give a word of wisdom, prophecy, or knowledge to those who need to be impacted by His love for them. He wants us to be believable, so when we share their issues and challenges with people, they will know only God can reveal the details of their lives to us. I invite you to pray this prayer with me:

Father God, help me to be believable so others may hear the good news of Your Son's birth, death, burial, and resurrection, and believe that You love them and came to save them, in Jesus' name.

Credible

We must become credible witnesses for our King. We must also be authentic in our faith and dependable in our service to God. When we looked at the life of Hezekiah, we saw that, at one time, he was credible in his faith and devoted to God. He was credible when he called the people back to worship the One True and Living God.

He understood God's blessings came along with His presence, so he reconnected the people to God through worship. As the people worshiped and adored God, He descended in their midst. His glory filled the temple, and the people received deliverance, healing, and blessings. All His goodness and blessings come with Him whenever and wherever God appears.

HEZEKIAH SHOWED the people that worshiping the King

was the key to obtaining prosperity, and they prospered greatly. Hezekiah was credible in his faith because he reestablished God in His rightful place and caused the people to focus once again on their faithful Helper.

A credible person is trustworthy and reliable, and they are known to follow through on what they say and have established themselves with a good reputation among their peers. A credible person does not put their hope in worldly things but in God, who is the supplier of all things. Think about the following passage of Scripture.

> TEACH *those who are rich in this world not to be proud and not to trust in their money, which is so unreliable. Their trust should be in God, who richly gives us all we need for our enjoyment. Tell them to use their money to do good. They should be rich in good works and generous to those in need, always being ready to share with others. By doing this they will be storing up their treasure as a good foundation for the future so they may experience true life.*
> —1Timothy 6:17-19 (NLT)

TIMOTHY WARNS those who are rich to watch their attitude because wealth can be unreliable and not bring credibility. He warns us not to be proud because we are financially blessed but to use these blessings to help those in need. God gives us wealth to fulfill His purposes on earth. Credible people understand the reason for wealth and are not haughty or high-minded because they are wealthy. These people think of others and help them because they know God is their Source, not their wealth.

If you and I put our hope in riches and not God, we are planting in unknown soil. Hezekiah started with great credibility but ended up proud and boastful. This is why he never took the opportunity to share about God with the king's messengers who visited him; instead, he showed them all the wealth he had obtained. Hezekiah forgot his wealth came from God and neglected to point the messengers to Him. Conduct a quick inventory of your life. How credible would those closest to you say you are?

Loyal

A loyal person is trustworthy. This person is dedicated to what they believe. They are faithful, committed, true to who they are, and devoted to their cause. They will remain steadfast in whatever position they have taken. A loyal person reflects the attributes of God. God is loyal and faithful to us even when we are unfaithful to Him. His love for us remains steadfast regardless of our struggles. His love and His compassion are constant and unchanging. No sin so great that it will change God's love and faithfulness toward you. This is why a person who may be sitting on death row can repent of their sins, and God will instantly forgive and provide them with eternal life. He is loyal, faithful, and steadfast in His devotion to His children.

WHILE WE ARE STRAYING from His narrow path, God remains steadfast in His commitment to change our hearts and lives if we ask Him. Are you loyal to God? As you look at the priorities of your 'life,' is God first, or does He fall below your family, work, friends, or hobbies? I want to share one of my favorite Scriptures with you because it speaks to our hearts about how loyalty should appear. "Therefore, my beloved brethren, be ye steadfast, unmovable, always abounding in the work of the Lord, forasmuch as ye know that your labor is not in vain in the Lord" (1 Corinthians 15:58 KJV).

A loyal person is steadfast, secure, and firm in their devotion. They are faithful workers and not easily dissuaded. Loyal people are committed to their assignment because they understand they are laboring for the Lord. This person understands sacrifice and is willing to give their life, if necessary, to please God.

MOTHER TERESA WAS A LOYAL PERSON. She was devoted to God and His call on her life and did not deviate from it despite her trials or difficulties. Mother Teresa remained steadfast when faced with the needs of the poor, those with deadly diseases, and the brokenness she saw all around her. She poured God's love into every person she met because of her loyalty and devotion to Him and the assignment He had given her. Her belief speaks to us of her passion and commitment to God and her trustworthiness in following Him wherever He led her.

MOTHER TERESA, I, and others have found as we faithfully serve God, He rewards us with peace, joy, hope, favor, and many blessings. The following quotes from **Mother Teresa** will inspire you to finish the course God has laid before you by being faithful, believable, credible, and loyal.

"DON'T LOOK for big things; just do small things with great love... The smaller the thing, the greater must be our love."

"BE FAITHFUL in small things because it is in them that your strength lies."

"BEING UNWANTED, unloved, uncared for, and forgotten by everybody, I think that is a much greater hunger, a much greater poverty than the person who has nothing to eat."

"DO NOT THINK THAT LOVE, in order to be genuine, has to be extraordinary. What we need is to love without getting tired."

"DO NOT WAIT FOR LEADERS; do it alone, person to person."

"EVEN THE RICH are hungry for love, for being cared for, for being wanted, for having someone to call their own."

"EVERY TIME you smile at someone, it is an action of love, a gift to that person, a beautiful thing. "

"GOD DOESN'T REQUIRE us to succeed; He only requires that you try."

"I TRY to give to the poor people for love what the rich could get for money. No, I wouldn't touch a leper for a thousand pounds; yet I willingly cure him for the love of God."

"I do not pray for success, I ask for faithfulness."

— *Mother Teresa*

A trustworthy heart asks:

Do I keep my promises?
Am I a person of my word?
Do I follow through on my commitments?
Am I reliable?
Am I honest?
Do I operate with integrity?
Can I be trusted?
Do I strive to resist temptation?

Whatever Your Answers to these questions are, ask God to change your heart so you can become more like His Son. We all have room for improvement and understanding what it means to be trustworthy will help us reconnect to God.

CHAPTER 7
A HUMBLE HEART

In my early twenties, I attended an event and received a word of wisdom and exhortation from someone I had just met. He said, "God has a great plan for your life, but remember to clothe yourself with humility."

I did not realize this was a Scripture at the time, but his words have stayed with me throughout my life and constantly reminded me to stay humble before the Lord and people.

To talk about humility is to talk about the life of Jesus and the example He has given to us. Jesus vividly modeled humility for us. He who is equal with God laid aside His glory and splendor, thus shedding His divine nature, to be born of a woman so He could redeem us. The Scripture says, "And being found in fashion as a man, he humbled himself and became obedient unto death, even the death of the cross" (Philippians 2:8 KJV).

As I reflect on Jesus' sacrifice, I am reminded God the Father clothed Himself in human flesh and came to us in the form of His Son. I want you to grasp this truth: The King of the universe came to live in one of His creations for nine months so that we could have oneness and a relationship with Him. For nine months, He was nourished in the womb of His mother, Mary, and after He was born, she took care of His daily needs. She breastfed Him (no baby formula during that century) and changed His diapers. She and her husband, Joseph, instructed Jesus and guided Him as He grew.

What Jesus did is humility in its most profound form. Jesus emptied Himself of His heavenly status, temporarily relinquished His power, and took on the form of a human to save us.

In heaven, Jesus humbled Himself to become a man, and while on earth, He humbled Himself and went to the cross. Humility gave His death value, the critical ingredient that will allow us to attain the blessings the Lord wants to impart into our lives. Humility is the secret of Jesus' atoning blood because, without it, He would never have gone to the cross. Humility is the source of our redemption and the reason we are free. Humility comes from the Latin word "humilis," which means low and humble, from the earth. To be humble is to be unpretentious, modest and not to think of ourselves as better than others. It causes us to be temperate in our dealings with people. Humility causes us to examine who we are so we do not become too self-important. It teaches us to be open-minded to learn things and gain wisdom, even from a child. A humble person is submitted to God and all authorities He institutes. They recognize the talents and virtues of other people and give honor where honor is due. They respect other people's skills, even when those talents and abilities far exceed their own because they willingly accept the gifts God has given to them. These people recognize their limitations and will not try to reach for what is beyond their grasp.

Pride and humility are in a constant struggle to possess us, and until Jesus becomes the Lord of our lives and takes center stage in our hearts, we will remain in this struggle. We can win this struggle if we take the example of Jesus and model our lives after the humility He so clearly demonstrated for us. Humbleness will enable us to go more than halfway to meet the needs of others.

Be Clothed with Humility

Many years after the gentleman told me to be clothed with humility, I came across the actual Scripture in 1 Peter 5, "Likewise, ye younger, submit yourselves unto the elder. Yea, all of you be subject to one another and be clothed with humility: for God resisteth the proud, but giveth grace to the humble. Humble, therefore, yourselves under the mighty hand of God, that he may exalt you in due time: casting all your care upon him; for he careth for you" (1 Peter 5:5-7 KJV).

To be clothed with humility means to dress in humility daily. You decide to put it on, so you are ready to handle it with grace and forgiveness no matter what you face in life. Humility is an attitude of the heart that allows us to walk in submission. As you clothe yourself with it, you can treat people with respect regardless of their position or status in life.

Over the years, I have traveled to many cities and stayed in some beautiful resorts. God reminded me of the value of small and great people while I was at a resort in Cape Cod. My group and I were hurrying to attend a meeting when the cleaning lady was trying to enter our suite. None of us paid her any attention. I was the last person to leave the room, and before I went out the door, I felt a prompting from the Holy Spirit to stop and acknowledge the woman.

I was immediately reminded that every person is valuable to God, no matter their station or vocation. God sees them through the eyes of grace, and so should we. I paused, turned around, said good morning, and thanked her for all her help. While this brought a huge smile to her face, it changed me profoundly. From that day forward, I have made a point of speaking to everyone, whether they are serving us or not. Humility causes us to value what God values, and He values people.

God did not send Jesus to die for things but for people. The things we have obtained do not have the same value as a human's life. The people we consider the least in society have been marked with God's handprint and sent to earth to fulfill a purpose. As we clothe ourselves with humility, we are reminded Jesus saved us from our sinful nature by becoming a servant for mankind.

Humility speaks to us about denying our own selfish needs so that we can become disciples of Jesus. Clothing ourselves with humility means we put on holiness and display Christ to everyone around us. It speaks of having a meek heart and a desire to pursue Jesus so that we can look more like Him. When you clothe yourself in any garment, it surrounds you; therefore, to be clothed with humility means the presence of the Lord covers you, and in His presence, you will always find divine favor and joy. Are you walking in humility before God? Do you wear humility daily as a mantle reflecting His presence in your life?

Humility in the Life of Believers

And whosoever shall exalt himself shall be abased; and he that shall humble himself shall be exalted.
—Matthew 23:12 (KJV)

JESUS TELLS us that if we humble ourselves, we will be exalted. This means we will be promoted, given more significant positions, and will receive an increase of God's blessings in our lives. As children of the world, we inherited our pride from Adam, but as believers in Jesus, we inherit our humility from Him. He is the only one who can make us truly humble.

JESUS TOLD His disciples He did not come into the world to be served but to serve people. His humility in us causes us to treat people with respect, love, honor, and dignity. When we acknowledge we can do nothing in our own strength and power, God will begin to dispense His love and humility through each of us. As we start to love our brothers and sisters sacrificially, we demonstrate God's love in the world. Our love for God is measured by our love for each other, as seen in Scripture. "He who does not love his brother whom he has seen, how can he love God whom he has not seen" (1 John 4:20). The humility we show to one another will prove that our humility before God is real and genuine.

TRUE HUMILITY IS NOT DEMONSTRATED in how we pray or in our daily devotional with God but in how we live each day to glorify and honor Him. How humble are you in your unguarded moments when no one is looking?

Humility is proof of our righteousness. Through humility, we demonstrate we have the right standing with God. Helen Keller said, "I long to accomplish a great and noble task, but it is my chief duty to accomplish humble tasks as though they were great and noble." Humility says, "Not me first, but you are first."

THE STORY of King Saul gives us a clear example of a person who started out being humble but whose humility turned to dust. Saul began his journey and service to the Lord with a pure heart. He considered himself the least in his family line and hid when God chose him to be the king over His people, but his heart later became corrupted, as is recorded in the Bible.

THEN THE WORD *of the LORD came to Samuel: "I am grieved that I have made Saul king, because he has turned away from me and has not carried out my instructions." Samuel was troubled, and he cried out to the LORD all that night. Early in the morning Samuel*

got up and went to meet Saul, but he was told, "Saul has gone to
Carmel. There he has set up a monument in his own honor and has
turned and gone on down to Gilgal." When Samuel reached him,
Saul said, "The LORD bless you! I have carried out the LORD's
instructions. But Samuel said, "What then is this bleating of sheep
in my ears? What is the lowing of cattle that I hear?" Saul
answered, "The soldiers brought them from the Amalekites; they
spared the best of the sheep and cattle to sacrifice to the Lord your
God, but we totally destroyed the rest." "Stop!" Samuel said to
Saul. "Let me tell you what the Lord said to me last night." "Tell
me," Saul replied. Samuel said, "Although you were once small in
your own eyes, did you not become the head of the tribes of Israel?
The LORD anointed you king over Israel. And he sent you on a
mission, saying, 'Go and completely destroy those wicked people,
the Amalekites; make war on them until you have wiped them out.'
Why did you not obey the LORD? Why did you pounce on the
plunder and do evil in the eyes of the LORD?" "But I did obey the
LORD," Saul said. "I went on the mission the LORD assigned me.
I completely destroyed the Amalekites and brought back Agag their
king. The soldiers took sheep and cattle from the plunder, the best of
what was devoted to God, in order to sacrifice them to the LORD
your God at Gilgal." But Samuel replied: Does the LORD delight
in burnt offerings and sacrifices as much as in obeying the voice of
the LORD? To obey is better than sacrifice, and to heed is better
than the fat of rams.
For rebellion is like the sin of divination (witchcraft), and arrogance
like the evil of idolatry. Because you have rejected the word of the
LORD, he has rejected you as king."
—1 Samuel 15:10-23 (NIV)

SAUL COMPLETELY LOST his relationship with God because of disobedience. He felt he had obeyed the instructions given to him by God, but he had not. God told him to destroy the Amalekites because, without any provocation, they had attacked the Israelites as they were coming out of Egyptian bondage. His instructions were to wipe out all the Amalekites and everything that belonged to them, including men, women, children, and animals.

Unfortunately, in gross error and lack of understanding, Saul kept their king and some of the best animals alive. Saul tried to reason with Samuel, saying he and his men had saved the best of the animals to sacrifice to God. If Saul had been thinking clearly, he would have realized God would not accept the sacrifice of animals that He had told him to destroy. Saul was afraid of the people, and he allowed them to influence him to the point where he sinned against God. Saul did not understand the severe consequences he would suffer from his disobedience, so he followed the people's advice and ignored God's instructions.

SAUL'S DISOBEDIENCE GRIEVED GOD, so God chose to remove the kingship and kingdom from him. Samuel had difficulty with God's decision and grieved over Saul, and he remembered how humble Saul was before his promotion and acquisition of the throne. Even though he was sad about Saul's demise, Samuel completely obeyed God's wishes when he confronted Saul. Saul repented and told Samuel he was afraid of the people and had given in to their demands, but God did not relent nor change His mind about removing Saul as king. I believe God decided because He knew Saul's heart and could see things in his heart that would have caused him to continue walking in disobedience. Even though Saul repented, God still took the kingdom from him.

SAUL BEGGED Samuel to forgive him and to come and worship God with him, but Samuel refused. Did you notice Saul repented to Samuel and asked for Samuel's forgiveness instead of God's? It is evident Saul was no longer in touch with the One who forgives sins; his heart had shifted away from God after he became king. Saul's heart was no longer pure and open to God. The Bible says that as the prophet Samuel turned to leave, Saul caught his robe in desperation, and it tore in his hand. Immediately the Word of the Lord to Saul was swift and powerful. Samuel said to Saul, "The Lord has torn the kingdom of Israel from you today and has given it to one of your neighbors -- to one who is better than you" (1 Samuel 15:28). God gave the kingdom to a person who was more humble and who would seek Him even when he sinned and missed God's standard.

SAUL'S JOURNEY had started well. He was humble before the Lord at the beginning, but his position as king, fear of the people, and lack of continued fellowship with God diminished his humility and caused him to stray from God's assignment. Saul discovered God does not delight in our sacrifices but prefers we obey His directives. God desires people to obey Him rather than try to please Him with gifts and sacrifices.

Disobedience and rebellion are likened to the sin of witchcraft; they lead to stubbornness, which God compares to idolatry (1 Samuel 15:23). Saul not only lost his position as king but became mentally unstable when God removed His presence from his life. He neglected to live in humility and obedience to God, and his life spiraled out of control. Saul didn't die a hero's death but the death of a coward because he failed to fulfill his God-given assignment.

BENEFITS OF HUMILITY

THERE ARE benefits for those of us who choose to walk in humility and please God:

You will enjoy an abundance of peace
(Psalm 37:11).

The Lord will increase your joy (Isaiah 29:19).
You will receive wisdom from God
(Proverbs 11:2).

Riches, honor, and life will be yours
(Proverbs 22:4).

God will give grace to the humble
(Proverb 3:34).

God will hear your desire (Psalm 10:17).

God will guide you with justice and teach you His ways
(Psalm 25:9).

God will lift you up, exalt you, and give you honor
(Psalm 147:6).

God will revive your spirit (Isaiah 57:15).

TO BE humble means constantly learning, being open to instruction, and walking in obedience. You will gain a deeper, richer relationship with God as you do these things. Not walking in humility means your heart is hardened and your mind is closed to the opportunities presented for your growth and development. A lack of humility keeps you from impacting the lives of people around you. When you are clothed with humility, you acknowledge God created you not to glorify yourself but to please Him and to help others. Humility causes us to recognize the dignity in each person God created. In our walk of humility, we can turn enemies into allies. To be humble does not mean you deny who you are; it allows you to become all God created you to be—a blessing to everyone you meet.

WHAT IS the state of your humility? Are you wholly clothed in it? Do not miss opportunities to live as Jesus lived —completely clothed in humility.

CHAPTER 8
A COURAGEOUS HEART

God has called us to be courageous people. The Scripture says He has not only given us power but love and soundness of mind to ensure our success.

s we examine 1 John 4:18 in its entirety, we see love is the antidote for keeping fear at bay. "There is no fear in love, but perfect love casts out fear because fear involves torment. But he who fears has not been made perfect in love." but perfect love casts out fear because fear involves torment. But he who fears has not been made perfect in love." God's perfect love for us and our response to His love keeps us steady when life seems to be swaying out of control. When we accept and embrace God's love, we understand He is a good Father who loves us and would never harm one of His children. This does not mean we will not encounter storms, but He is with us to bring about our deliverance in the storms. Storms, worries, and fear are all from the devil and are intended for our harm. God's perfect love is available and reminds us of what the enemy means for evil in our lives; God will turn around for our good (Romans 8:28).

Love for the Savior, the One who paid an exorbitant price for us, can fill us with courage. Stephen's love for Jesus certainly made him brave and courageous, even as he was stoned to death for preaching the gospel of Christ with boldness and passion. He was fearless in telling others who Jesus was and what He accomplished for us through His death. Stephen dared to defy the Pharisees by reminding them of how they had plotted and killed God's Son, and he was valiant and dauntless in the face of death.

To be a person of courage, you and I must not allow ourselves to be overtaken by fear. In 1 John 4:18, we see why love is the antidote to fear: "Perfect love casts out fear." Love made Stephen fearless!

Second Timothy reveals that fear does not have its root in God. "For God did not give us a spirit of timidity, but a spirit of power, love, and self-discipline" (2 Timothy 1:7 NLT). God did not put fear in the hearts of His children, so the root of fear comes from the devil. God has given us a deposit of His Holy Spirit, who causes us to be bold and courageous in the battles we face. You will not find timidity in the Godhead, and no timidity should be found in you. God deposited power, love, and a sound mind into us. God has given us power, which means He has given us strength, might, force, influence, and authority. When you are faced with a situation, that causes you to be fearful and to lack courage, you must remind yourself of the deposit of courage God made in you to combat the onslaught of fear. Someone defined fear as "false evidence appearing real." Fear seems real, but it is not.

I was scheduled for a business trip to Chicago after the attacks on September 11. A few days before my departure, another plane crashed because it was too close to the jet wash of an aircraft in front of it. Fear gripped me so severely that I thought I would have a heart attack. On my way to the airport, I prayed, sang, worshipped, petitioned, and begged God for peace. As I took my seat, the Holy Spirit kept reminding me to be at peace because all was well. However, I was so wholly gripped with fear that although I heard Him, I could not find peace. The gentleman sitting next to me did not help much because he went to the restroom three times before the plane's takeoff.

Generally, I enjoy takeoffs, but as the plane taxied down the runway, the Holy Spirit shouted at me to get a hold of me. Worry and fear had me in their grip, and my heart was pounding. The fear of the plane crashing seemed so real, but it was not real. The plane did not crash, nor did any incidents happen on the flight. What I experienced stemmed entirely from fear. I almost caused a heart attack because I believed in a lie from the devil. The enemy had created a stronghold in my mind with his lies about the plane crashing. I completely blocked out the voice of the Holy Spirit before and after I boarded the flight. My mind was so wrapped in fear the voice of the Holy Spirit could not penetrate it.

I learned a few things that day: it is impossible for the

devil to tell the truth and for the Holy Spirit to lie. Unfortunately, many believe the devil lies over the Holy Spirit's truth. Fear had me swimming downstream, grasping frantically to stay at peace while the truth of the Holy Spirit, and the Word of God concerning peace, should have kept me at rest and in a secure place in Him. I also discovered that many things we worry about and lose sleep over would never happen to us. Some people have become ill because of worry and fear. It has been proven that only eight percent of the things we fear will ever happen to us. This means ninety-two percent of what you are worried about, or lacking courage will never occur.

God has deposited within every believer the power to have self-control and self-discipline. We can discipline our emotions to respond to the truth of God's Word and not react to the enemy's lies. Unfortunately, as I did, many people will more readily accept the lies about their difficult circumstances rather than the truth that God has the answer for each difficulty. When God's perfect love is operating in your life, fear cannot stay. As fear tries to enter your heart, love reminds you God dwells in you, and there is no room to harbor it. The Scripture tells us fear brings torment when it arrives. I can attest to this. Several weeks before the trip to Chicago, I was so harassed by fear and doubt that I would have given it if I had a valid reason to give my boss not to fly. I realized I was in the grip of fear but felt powerless to overcome it, even though I was not helpless at all. The enemy taunted and tormented me, and I allowed him to do it.

The Scripture says we are not made perfect in love when

we fear. This means fear keeps us from experiencing whole-ness in our relationship with God. Fear keeps us from trusting Him and leaves us struggling in the face of false evidence about our situation, which is what the enemy wants. What happened to my courage in the face of fear? I had none. I had lost my connection to God because of fear. In my panic, I was not allowing the Holy Spirit to reconnect me to my Source of love, peace, and protection. God wants you to have a sound mind free from fear, worry, and anxiety.

The Apostle Paul wrote a letter to Timothy at a time in his life when fear had gripped him severely because Nero's secret police wanted to kill him. Fear had taken a firm grip on Timothy's heart, and Paul wrote to reconnect him to God and bring peace to his soul. Paul wanted to steady Timothy in the trials he was facing by reminding Him God was an ever-present help in times of trouble (Psalm 46:1).

Paul encouraged Timothy to keep a sound mind, which means to be saved and to be delivered. Paul was saying to Timothy then and to us, today, "Take courage in the midst of crisis." Paul had experienced many difficult seasons in his Christian walk where God had to deliver, rescue, revive, salvage, and protect him. Because of these experiences, he could encourage Timothy and us. God will deliver us safe and sound to His destination for us, even though the storms may be raging out of control. He will salvage our minds and emotions from the onslaught of the enemy. When your mind wants to succumb to fear, or your courage fails, the Word of God is all you need. The Holy Spirit is your rescuer, and He will be with you every step of the way. A person of courage will grab hold of God's Word and hold on tightly to it when fear tries to overrun their heart. This very act requires boldness.

Boldness

To be courageous speaks of being bold, which means to be audacious, forward-thinking, have nerve, be ready at any moment, and advance. Do any of these definitions describe you—all the time? If not, then journey with me to find help from the Word to fortify us for the race ahead.

> *For I fully expect and hope that I will never be ashamed, but that I will continue to be bold for Christ, as I have been in the past. And I trust that my life will bring honor to Christ, whether I live or die. For to me, living means living for Christ, and dying is even better. But if I live, I can do more fruitful work for Christ. So I really don't know which is better. I'm torn between two desires: I long to go and be with Christ, which would be far better for me. But for your sakes, it is better that I continue to live.*
> —Philippians 1:20-24 (NLT)

After reading these words from the Apostle Paul, are you wondering why you fear death? Paul tells us that in dying, we get to be with Christ. Paul was torn between two worlds. He desired to carry on his work and help as many people as possible come to the saving knowledge of Jesus Christ, but on the other hand, he also longed to be in the presence of the Lord. Paul experienced many trials on his Christian journey;

he was beaten, shipwrecked, imprisoned, and put in chains. Yet, through all these trials, he maintained his boldness for Christ and the gospel. Paul was audacious and had a lot of nerve, even when faced with life-threatening situations. He did not back down or hide from the opposition but was courageous and bold in his walk of faith.

Paul understood he was chained because of the gospel of Jesus Christ and his faith in that gospel, and he still boldly shared Christ with those who would listen. Paul's boldness displayed Christ and gave hope to others to keep persevering in the face of their trials.

When we are faced with a decision to be bold, we are often pulled in two directions. It feels like there is a force pulling you first one way and then the other. You might feel you are in a tug-of-war, which is precisely what is happening. Courage demands we stand for what we believe, even though it may be unpopular, while fear tells us we look stupid for taking a stand and will lose in the end.

Boldness means you stand firm and keep pressing toward your desired goal by trusting the results to God. It tells you to have the nerve to stand for what is right and just. Boldness denotes having a strong passion and strong emotions; when these feelings are in operation, nothing will stop you from acting. A bold person is consumed with what must be accomplished and does not sit idly waiting for things to happen but takes the necessary steps to get the ball rolling. Some people may look at a person who operates in boldness and label them foolish for being so bold or forward-thinking. When you are passionate about a cause, it is part of the destiny God birthed you to fulfill, and you must pour your all into accomplishing it.

Although Paul was small, he walked boldly and was firm in his thinking and beliefs. Before encountering the risen Christ on his way to Damascus, he was passionate and bold when persecuting Christians. When he met Christ, and his life was transformed, he became even more passionate, determined, and fearless in his desire to see people's lives changed and connected with the Savior. A bold person is ready at any moment to move forward and will advance no matter what struggles they are facing. They understand the results may not always be favorable, but their passion for the cause keeps them pressing toward the goal.

Both the Apostle Paul and Stephen were passionate about Christ. They did not shrink back when they faced roadblocks or when their lives were threatened. They kept speaking, moving forward, and keeping the vision alive. They were determined to reconnect those lost to an intimate relationship with their Father. They understood there was no other way to the Father but through the Son, Jesus, and though many Jews did not accept this, they kept sharing the gospel of truth. They lived with courage and passion, and they died heroic deaths. Our boldness for Christ will come under scrutiny by people and the devil. Therefore, we must model ourselves after the examples of Christ and others who have paved the way for us and shown us how to live courageously.

To Be Daring

A daring person is someone brave and courageous when faced with difficulties. They stand firm while being tried in the fires of adversity. Jesus was fearless and courageous, and the Bible says He set His face like flint and went all the way to the cross of Calvary for you and me. Stephen also exemplified great daring and courage as he faced death. Because both Jesus and Stephen were daring and determined, they fulfilled the challenging assignments God had given to them.

FOR THE LORD GOD will help me; therefore shall I not be confounded: therefore have I set my face like a flint, and I know that I shall not be ashamed.
—Isaiah 50:7 (KJV).

AND IT CAME TO PASS, when the time was come that he should be received up, he steadfastly set his face to go to Jerusalem.
—Luke 9:51 (KJV).

JESUS WAS COURAGE IN ACTION! He was daring, determined, and steadfast as He faced the trials, tribulations, and horrific death He came to planet Earth to accomplish on our behalf. Jesus knew what type of death He would face when He chose to go to earth and die in our place. He had watched the Roman crucifixion for centuries and knew the horrendous nature of the death He would suffer, but He still came to set us free.

LET me paint a clear picture of His courage and daring for

you. Remember, the Son of God reclothed Himself in human flesh so that He could rescue us. He left heaven, came to earth as a baby, and lived for nine months in the belly of one of His creations. Jesus stripped Himself of all authority and submitted His will to His earthly parents so He could die in our place. He then spent thirty years being trained, tried, and tested before God allowed him to walk into the fullness of His destiny. He had to wait on God's divine timing patiently. Many centuries before, the Prophet Isaiah had prophesied that when it was His time to give His life, He would set His face like a flint all the way to Jerusalem. Jesus journeyed to Jerusalem, knowing this was not the end but our new beginning.

FROM THE MOMENT He began fulfilling His purpose, Jesus was daring and confrontational in His relationship with the Jews. He challenged their faith, tested their beliefs, and did things such as healing and setting people free on the Sabbath day, which the religious leaders claimed was against their laws. In all this, He was attempting to awaken them from their spiritual slumber. They became so steeped in their religious traditions and doctrines that when the very One whose appearance they had been waiting for did come, they did not recognize Him. Jesus did not fit their mold or preconceived ideas of what the Messiah would be like or what He would do when He appeared.

THE JEWS ATTEMPTED to trap Jesus many times so they could kill Him but were unsuccessful in their attempts. Jesus continued His radical ministry for three years. Although He healed the sick, raised the dead, cleansed the lepers, and set the captives free, these miracles still did not cause a change in the hearts of many of the religious Jews. Jesus spent time in the garden of Gethsemane praying, preparing to die, and be resurrected. He poured out His heart to God, saying, "O my Father, if it be possible, let this cup pass from me: nevertheless, not as I will, but as thou wilt" (Matthew 26:39).

As I stated before, Jesus knew the nature of the death He would endure. I don't believe the fear of dying on the cross led Him to pray for release. Jesus knew when He hung on the cross, all the sins of mankind would be laid upon Him. He also understood that a Holy God could not be in the presence of sin, so He expected the Father to turn away the instant He *took* on our sins. In the eons of time Jesus had existed with the Father, He had never once experienced separation from God. I believe Jesus asked for the cup to be removed because He did not want to be separated from His Father.

In Matthew 27, the Bible says as He hung on the cross, darkness covered the land, and Jesus cried with a loud voice, "Eli, Eli lamsa-bach-thani?" He said, "My God, My God, why hast thou forsaken me?" God's presence was removed, the light was replaced with darkness, and Jesus felt abandoned by God. You and I often think God has abandoned us because we are going through tough times. Even though Jesus felt the absence of His Father, God had not forsaken Him. Our sins laid on Him caused God's presence to be removed from Him until after the resurrection. God is with us in our darkest moments, too. God is our Father, and He loves us as much as He loves Jesus.

He does not abandon us in our distress. Though Jesus felt

forsaken and abandoned by His Father, God was waiting for the right moment when He could raise His precious Son from the dead. This He did three days later. Jesus was sinless, but our sins caused Him to suffer the agony of a time of separation from His Father. Yet, His courage was remarkable as He faced death, hell, and the grave. Without His sacrifice, we would be helpless and hopeless.

ISAIAH 50 PAINTS a picture of Jesus as He journeyed toward the cross. He knew God was watching and monitoring each step He took. Jesus understood God was His helper, and there was nothing to fear with God by His side. God would not allow Him to be disgraced for placing His trust in Him. Because Jesus knew God could be trusted to raise Him from the dead at the appointed time, He positioned Himself to win on our behalf. He was determined and daring, giving Him the confidence to set His face like flint and step into the destiny He was born to fulfill.

To SET His face like flint means He determinedly set His face toward the situation. He hardened Himself like stone. He was immovable in His determination and durable in His faith, which was the fuel that propelled Him to the cross. His faith kept Him steady as He walked the difficult path to Golgotha's hill. He was courageous and determined, and when He left His Throne in Heaven, He understood His sacrifice would bring our salvation. He set His face toward the cross, endured the pain and suffering, and prevailed!

Having Confidence

People with confidence know who they are, understand who they serve, and operate with the courage to become more than conquerors. When you are confident, you are self-assured and filled with faith. You think positively and operate in trust. God rewards us for our faith, hope, trust, and confidence in Him. "Cast not away, therefore, your confidence, which hath great recompense of reward. For ye have need of patience, that after ye have done the will of God, ye might receive the promise." (Hebrews 10:35-36 KJV).

THE PASSAGE above assures us that having confidence in God brings blessings to our lives. It also challenges us not to throw away our confidence. We must choose to hold fast to what we believe. We can choose to hold fast to our beliefs or let life's delays, difficulties, and frustrations cause us to throw away what we are hoping for and miss the reward God has for us.

Even as I write this segment, I believe some of you may struggle with giving up because your journey is so difficult. You might be overcome with discouragement because the waiting season has been unending. Others may feel overwhelmed by how difficult things have been and have grown weary of encouraging themselves in the Lord. On many occasions, I have had to declare the promises of God out loud. I did this to remind myself of the blessings God has in store for me if I don't lose confidence in His ability to deliver on His promises.

ONE MORNING, as I greeted the Father and thanked Him

for a new day, I felt discouragement trying to settle over me like a blanket. I had to declare out loud I would not let discouragement steal my joy, and as I began to pray, I had to battle hard to keep myself from giving in to it. I searched the Bible for encouraging scriptures and began to declare out loud some of the promises for my life from God's Word. It took over an hour before the feelings subsided, and I then spent time in praise and worship to solidify my position of trusting in God's faithfulness. I had almost lost confidence in God's ability because the waiting season had been so long and intense, but God helped me to hold on to Him as He lifted me out of the pit that was prepared for me by the devil. God will also lift you out of the pit of despair if you cling tightly to His promises.

GOD IS mindful of the confidence you have placed in Him. He sees the time, love, support, and energy you have invested in your service to Him and will repay you for your faithfulness. When you commit to accomplishing the assignment given to you, God will not do less for you than your earthly employer. He will repay you for every seed you have planted in the Kingdom's work and people's lives. If your earthly employer pays you a good salary for your work, then God will pay you even more for your work for Him.

God rewards your confidence in Him. He never overlooks the sacrifices, long hours, and how you have poured your heart and soul into every assignment. He will never forget your labor of love. The key is to be patient. Patience is necessary because sometimes the rewards are delayed for a season, but they will come if you keep hoping and waiting in faith.

GOD WILL REWARD you in many ways. He will ensure your victory, cause you to prosper and succeed, increase the anointing in your life as you press into Him during difficult seasons, and give you double for your trouble. Your faith and confidence will pay off big! God keeps excellent records and pays great dividends. Commit to maintaining your trust, even when you cannot see how He will provide.

As I wait on God and keep believing for His promises to manifest in my life, I say to Him, "I don't know how but I know Who; I don't know when, but I know where." I believe God will manifest His promises in your life even though you don't know when they will arrive. Hold on to Him and refuse to give up on the seeds you have planted in the Kingdom of God. They are grown in good soil and will produce an abundant harvest in your life. Do not give up! Hold on to your confidence in God because it pays great dividends.

A Heart of Grace

We discovered many things as we looked closely at what it means to be courageous. Courage comes from a heart that is committed and sold out to Christ. Since your heart is the center, the substance of your life, God has poured His love and grace into you. Grace means to be courteous and compassionate and to show mercy. Colossians 3 describes a heart filled with grace.

SINCE GOD CHOSE you to be the holy people he loves, you must clothe yourselves with tenderhearted mercy, kindness, humility,

gentleness, and patience. Make allowance for each other's faults, and forgive anyone who offends you. Remember, the Lord forgave you, so you must forgive others. Above all, clothe yourselves with love, which binds us all together in perfect harmony. And let the peace that comes from Christ rule in your hearts. For as members of one body you are called to live in peace. And always be thankful.
—Colossians 3:12-15 (NLT)

To have a heart filled with grace means you are gentle, holy, humble, kind, merciful, patient, and tender. You represent all these things when you are courageous because your total dependency is on the Lord. Since Jesus embodies gentleness, holiness, humility, kindness, mercy, patience, and tenderness, He has deposited these seeds into every person who has asked Him to be their Savior.

To be graceful and kind in our dealings with others, we must live in holiness, focus our hearts on doing holy things, live in truth, and be sure our lives are hidden in Christ. As we do this, we will not become fault finders but love unconditionally and extend compassion to those struggling with life.

Scripture encourages us to forgive anyone who offends us. This is most important because the enemy traps us into taking offense and keeps us rehearsing the injustice until it becomes poison in our souls. If our souls get contaminated, our whole life is poisoned. To keep your soul clean, you must not give in to the offense. Acknowledge the wrong has occurred and choose to release it to God as you forgive the offender. Grace always points us toward love. Although we do not deserve the grace, God so lavishly poured out on us through His Son, love still provided the grace. Grace saw us in our sin and came to our rescue, not because we earned or deserved rescuing, but because the grace of God would not leave us broken and in ruins.

As you and I allow the grace of God to become the compass for our lives, we will begin to live in peace and harmony with each other. This, in turn, will allow us to live in unity, which is the place where God pours out His blessings.

HERE ARE some keys to having a heart filled with grace:

God wants you to love one another.

God dearly loves you and has poured His grace into your heart.

Dress yourselves daily with compassion and love.

Allow kindness to rule your life.

Clothe yourself with humility.

Be gentle and harmless when dealing with others.

Walk in patience.

Bear each other's burdens by encouraging, exhorting, building, and lifting one another up.

As you and I apply these keys to our lives, we will be blessed and be a beacon of hope to those who are lost. Courage calls us to be as bold as a lion and as tender as a lamb. We can face each situation bravely because we are never alone; God is with us each step of the way. Let your heart overflow with the compassion, love, and grace of our Lord Jesus Christ.

CHAPTER 9
A YIELDED HEART

To be yielded means to surrender all. The song "All to Jesus I Surrender," by Judson Van Deventer, speaks of a life that is totally yielded to God. When you are surrendered, you are yielded to God and have abandoned yourself entirely into His care.

Y ou submit your heart to His plans and purposes and obey His every word. You will become pliable and usable as you yield in the Master's hands. Being surrendered to God causes you to produce great things in life because He will be able to use you to bring glory and honor to His name. In yielding, you desire to enthrone Jesus in your heart so He can give all honor and glory to the Father.

FOR I THROUGH the law am dead to the law, that I might live unto God. I am crucified with Christ: nevertheless I live; yet not I, but

Christ liveth in me: and the life which I now live in the flesh I live by the faith of the Son of God, who loved me, and gave himself for me. I do not frustrate the grace of God: for if righteousness cometh by the law, then Christ is dead in vain.
—Galatians 2:19-21 (KJV)

WHEN YOU READ this passage of Scripture, I hope you see a reflection of a person who has yielded and surrendered all to the Lordship of Jesus Christ. This person has ceased doing things of his own strength and has declared, "I give up." He has given up the struggle to survive on his own and realized he could not live apart from Jesus Christ. As we yield our lives to God, we, too, will live a life of faith anchored in the Son of God.

WHEN JESUS WAS CRUCIFIED, He was nailed to a cross. Therefore, to be crucified with Him means you and I must nail our fleshly needs and desires to the cross by walking in His footsteps daily. As you begin to live for Him, you allow His light to shine through you. The message in the Scripture is that the cross is the judgment seat for sin; therefore, Jesus' death on the cross fulfilled the law, which required the shedding of blood to set us free. Not only did Jesus bear our guilt and shame, but He also died the death we should have. He committed no sin of His own to warrant His death but was willing to take our place so that we could walk in the newness of life. When He died, all prior claims the devil had against us because of Adam and Eve's sin of disobedience were canceled. The cross is our coronation place where we let go of our selfish ambitions and enthrone the Lord Jesus

Christ. Jesus' death was unselfish, saying, "It is not about 'Me,' but it is all about you." He teaches us to let go of selfishness and be willing to make a difference in people's lives. As we surrender our lives to Him, we will begin to live each day to please Him and bring joy to His heart.

JUDSON VAN DEVENTER wrote the song, "All to Jesus I Surrender," in eighteen ninety-six as a testimony of his life. For years, Judson studied art; his entire life was pursuing it. He did not desire to be in Christian service because he dreamed of becoming an outstanding and famous artist. While in college, Van Deventer studied drawing and painting under a well-known German teacher. As he pursued his ambition of becoming a renowned artist, he taught art as a subject and became the Art Supervisor at a public school.

THE SPIRIT of God urged Van Deventer to enter the Evangelistic field one day when his church held a revival, but he would not yield. He still had a burning desire to be an artist. He battled against God and his calling for five years, but the time came when he could no longer hold out against God. Judson Van Deventer finally surrendered all to God. He surrendered his heart, time, gifts, and talents, and a new day dawned in his life. He had desired to become an artist through his drawings and paintings, but God wanted to make him an artist through his songs. When he yielded to God, God gave him the words to the song, "All to Jesus I Surrender," which has been sung in churches for centuries.

As Judson surrendered, he began living the Scripture in Galatians 2:20, which says it was no longer him living, but Christ was now living through him. You can see from the song's words that Judson discovered the true meaning of having a yielded heart and life.

ALL TO JESUS I SURRENDER; All to Him I freely give; I will ever love and trust Him, In His presence daily live. I surrender all, I surrender all; All to Thee, my blessed Savior, I surrender all. All to Jesus I surrender; humbly at His feet I bow, Worldly pleasures all forsaken; take me, Jesus, take me now. All to Jesus I surrender; Make me, Savior, wholly Thine; Let me feel Thy Holy Spirit, Truly know that Thou art mine. All to Jesus I surrender; Lord, I give myself to Thee; Fill me with Thy love and power; Let Thy blessing fall on me. All to Jesus I surrender; now I feel the sacred flame. Oh, the joy of full salvation! Glory, glory, to His Name!

GOD HAS DEPOSITED in our hearts gifts and talents He desires to use in His Kingdom. We often do not use our gifts and talents for His purposes because we have our plans and are unwilling to yield our wills and hearts to Him. We fail to realize that the gifts God has given us when used as He plans, will far exceed what we can accomplish on our own. His gifts will take us into places and before people, we cannot imagine or even comprehend. His gifts will make room for you wherever He sends you. His gifts will cause your name to be great. His gifts will show men the way back to the Father. If you have not yet yielded your heart or surrendered your plans to the governance of the Lord Jesus Christ, I encourage you not to waste another moment; do so now and then watch His greatness unfold in your life as His greatness grew in the life of Judson Van Deventer.

Abandonment

JUDSON VAN DEVENTER abandoned his plans to embrace those God had for his life. When you and I quit our plans, we can embrace all God has for us. I have met many people over the years with college degrees in specific areas of study, but in many cases, these people are not working in their field. What happened? As some of them matured, they discovered something else they wanted to do with their lives, so they abandoned their old plan to embrace a new one. Others could not find a job in their field of study, which forced them to go into an entirely different field.

After coming into a relationship with Jesus Christ, some discovered He had other plans for their lives, so they yielded to His plans. In each of these instances, the people surrendered their wills to the new thing being presented. Some of you have found new freedom in abandoning what you thought you would become and embracing something different. In the Scripture, we discover what true freedom is.

So if the Son sets you free, you are truly free
John 8:36 (NLT).

WHEN YOU AND I encountered the risen Son of God, and He came into our hearts, He freed us from the traps of the enemy and gave us a new life. As a result, we have learned how to abandon our lives into His care. We understand He governs all our affairs. Whatever existed in our hearts before Him living in us must leave. The Bible says light and darkness cannot exist together (2 Corinthians 6:14), so when Jesus, the Light, entered our hearts, all the darkness that once dwelt in us had to flee. The enemy will try to convince us at times that we have the same nature, but we must remind him the greater One lives and rules in us, and darkness cannot inhabit where He dwells.

JESUS SET US FREE, so we can have eternal life, praise, and worship Him, live in peace, and be filled daily with His joy. He has shown us how a life lived free from sin, shame, and guilt is possible through His shed blood. Jesus poured God's redemptive grace into our hearts, and along with this grace came God's abundant favor. He lights the pathway for us and ensures our safety. As we abandon ourselves to Him, He shows us how to live by experiencing freedom and liberty through the power of the Holy Spirit.

SOME OF YOU can remember how, as children, you enjoyed total freedom. You abandoned yourselves over to whatever childish games you were playing without a care in the world. You did this because you knew you were protected and provided for and trusted your parents to care for you. Jesus has come to set you free and invites you to abandon your cares to Him because He will protect and provide for you. You can trust your heart to His care.

WE MUST COME to a place in life where we decide whether we will surrender our ways to God's ways and our plans to His plans. When you get to this crossroad, remember that God's plans for your life are abundantly above all you can ask, think, or imagine (Ephesians 3:20). Whatever you have planned for yourself will never measure up to the greatness

He has in store for you. If you have not abandoned yourself to Christ, the question must be, "What is holding you back?" Abandon yourself to His care and watch as He begins to unfold His greatness in your life.

Obedience

A significant part of yielding is being obedient. We have always struggled with obedience because we are inherently rebellious by nature. We like to do things our way, in our own time and don't necessarily want to be told what to do by anyone, including God. Obedience is the key to true happiness, as it keeps us from making harmful decisions. Obedience speaks of loyalty and devotion. When we choose to obey God, we should obey without conditions. Partial obedience is not obedience at all. God desires our total obedience to His directives for our lives. As we learn to depend entirely on Him, we develop trust and confidence in His ability to direct our steps and provide for our daily needs. The more we trust Him, the more obedient we become. When we couple trusting God with obedience, we will discover what it means to be abundantly blessed, and everything we put our hands on will prosper and succeed.

THE STORY of Gideon in Judges 6 gives us a clear understanding of how obedience brings about victory in our lives.

AND THE ANGEL of the LORD appeared unto him, and said unto him, The LORD is with thee, though mighty man of valor. And Gideon said unto him, Oh my Lord, if the LORD be with us, why

then is all this befallen us? And where be all his miracles which our
fathers told us of, saying, Did not the LORD bring us up from
Egypt? but now the Lord hath forsaken us, and delivered us into the
hands of the Midianites. And the LORD looked upon him, and said,
Go in this thy might, and thou shalt save Israel from the hands of
the Midianites: have not I sent thee?
—Judges 6:12-14 (KJV)

GOD USED Gideon to free the Israelites from the oppression of the Midianites. The Midianites were enemies who raided Israel each year, taking their crops and goods. They would let their animals loose into the Israelites' fields, and their animals would devour and destroy their crops. When the Israelites resisted, they were driven into caves in the mountains and had to scavenge for food. The Israelites lost everything to the Midianites, including their houses, food, and goods; therefore, they lived like paupers, homeless and lost. God commissioned Gideon to fight on His behalf and to set His people free. Gideon was unsure of himself and fearful when God chose him.

When the angel approached him, the angel told Gideon the Lord was with him and that he was a mighty man of valor. Gideon did not see himself as powerful, and his response to the angel showed his image of himself. He told the angel he came from a low-income family and was the least in his household, which meant he had little value at home. Gideon failed to realize that God already had this insight into his background and how he felt about himself, and God saw him from a different perspective. God saw

Gideon as someone mighty and filled with strength, even though he was unaware these attributes were a part of him.

MANY TIMES before God can use us, He has to rewire our thinking about who we are and what we can accomplish for Him. Words have tremendous power, and the angel used them effectively to open Gideon's heart to the great opportunity that God was giving him to set His people free. It took convincing for Gideon to see himself as God saw him. Gideon wanted proof that this was a messenger from God and said so as he prepared a meal for the angel. When Gideon returned, the angel told him to place the meal on the altar and pour the broth over it. Using the staff he held, the angel touched the food on the altar, and fire came out of the rock and consumed it. This incident propelled Gideon to walk in faith and obedience, but he was still unsure whether God was with him.

LATER THAT NIGHT, the Lord appeared to him with his first assignment. Gideon was to tear down the altar of Baal the Israelites had built, construct an altar unto the Lord, and then sacrifice a bull on the altar to God. Baal was considered to be a Canaanite deity. His name meant lord and master, and the people considered him their provider. It was said Baal took care of the farms, flocks, and herds. He was also called the son of Dagon, who the Canaanites believed controlled the grain and the rain. They thought he was in total control; unfortunately, many Israelites also believed this. Baal had taken the place of the one true God in the hearts of many of His people.

GIDEON WAS fearful and decided to tear down Baal's altar at night with the help of ten of his friends. In the morning, when the people saw the altar of Baal thrown down, they demanded to know who had done it and discovered it was Gideon. They wanted to kill him, but God had other plans. The Spirit of the Lord came upon Gideon, and he became bold and gathered the people around him for the work of the Lord.

EVEN THOUGH GOD had proven Himself to Gideon, he still asked for other signs and decided to test God by fleecing Him. Gideon told God he would put a fleece of wool on the floor, and if the morning dew were only on the fleece and not on the floor, he would know God would use him to save the Israelites. God did as he asked, and the following morning, the fleece was saturated with water while the floor was dry. Still, Gideon wanted another sign. Gideon did not fleece God to know His will, for the angel had already told him God's will. The fleecing was a sign of his unbelief and a lack of trust in God.

GIDEON IS like many of us as it relates to trusting God. We know God is faithful to His Word, but often we are unsure He will move on our behalf. God has repeatedly proven that He will do what He has promised to do in our lives, but we are still fearful and timid, so we hesitate to move forward.

THE NEXT SIGN Gideon asked from the Lord was that the fleece would dry and the floor around the fleece would be wet with dew. This request was for a miracle because it would be contrary to nature. The following day God did as Gideon asked. The fleece was dry, and the floor was wet. Gideon was ready to obey the instructions of the Lord after this. He would still undergo testing along the way as he prepared to produce results for God. He was tested but obeyed and brought a tremendous harvest for the Kingdom.

Productivity

And the LORD said unto Gideon, the people are yet too many; bring them down unto the water, and I will try them for thee there: and it shall be, that of whom I say unto thee, This shall go with thee, the same shall go with thee; and of whomsoever I say unto thee, This shall not go with thee, the same shall not go. So he brought down the people unto the water: and the LORD said unto Gideon, Every one that lappeth of the water with his tongue, as a dog lappeth, him shalt thou set by himself; likewise everyone that boweth down upon his knees to drink. And the number of them that lapped, putting their hand to their mouth, were three hundred men: but all the rest of the people bowed downed upon their knees to drink water. And the LORD said unto Gideon, By the three hundred men that lapped will I save you, and deliver the Midianites into thine hand: and let all the other people go every man unto his place. So the people took victuals in their hand, and their trumpets: and he sent all the rest of Israel every man unto his tent, and retained those three hundred men: and the host of Midian was beneath him in the valley.
—Judges 7:4-8 (KJV)

WHEN YOU AND I yield to God, we become productive. We will produce a harvest that will yield fruit in the lives of others and bear fruit in our own lives. It is impossible to yield your heart to God, put action to your faith, and not produce results. We can only make a harvest by our willingness to work. As we look at the life of Gideon, we see he delivered great results for God because he yielded himself and obeyed God's instructions.

IN THE ABOVE SCRIPTURE, God gave further instructions to Gideon, which was additional training in obedience. Though Gideon was fearful and did not consider himself worthy of the assignment, he was able to amass 32,000 men to go to war against the Midianites because God was with him. God said there were too many men. God was concerned when the Israelites won the battle, they would think they were successful because of their strength, so He told Gideon to tell those who were fearful to go home. Twenty thousand men went home, leaving Gideon with 10,000. God then told Gideon that the remaining 10,000 were still too many and instructed him to bring them down to the water so He could test them.

WHEN THE MEN arrived at the brook, they started drinking the water. God told Gideon those who lapped the water with their tongue like a dog would be set aside. Those who bowed down on their knees to drink were to be sent home. This was an unusual test, but God understands the heart of man. God reduced the number of men because He was unwilling to let the people steal His glory for victory.

God wanted the nation to realize He was with them and to turn back to Him. Only 300 of the 10,000 men lapped the water and were allowed to go to war with Gideon. Those who lapped the water were alert and aware of what was happening around them and would be vigilant as they faced the enemy. Those who knelt were entirely focused on their needs and satisfying themselves and were unaware of the dangers around them as they battled. God chose those ready in and out of season to do His work.

GIDEON FOLLOWED GOD'S INSTRUCTIONS, even though he may not have understood how to win a war with only 300 men. Since he passed yet another test of obedience, God told him to go to the war, and he had already delivered the enemy into his hands. God knew Gideon still feared and doubted their success, so He instructed him to take his servant and go down to the enemy's camp to listen to their conversations. This strengthened Gideon for the war ahead.

When they arrived, Gideon saw the enemy, and their horses were as numerous as the sand on the seashore. As they listened to the conversation, one of the men shared a dream he had about a loaf of bread tumbling down in the tent of Midian and crushing them. The other man responded the dream was the sword of the Lord and Gideon because God had already delivered the Midianites into his hands. When Gideon heard the dream and the interpretation, he worshipped the Lord and returned to camp, ready to face the enemy. He told the men to prepare because God had delivered the enemy into their hands. They were fortified for battle and prepared to produce results for God.

GIDEON COULD ONLY BE successful because of his obedience to God's plans. He divided the men into groups, told them to blow the trumpets following his lead, and then used the words he had heard from the enemy's dream, *the sword of the Lord and Gideon.* God had put the words for victory into the mouth of the enemy. It was a Rhema word from God specifically for Gideon, and he used it effectively to get the victory.

OUR ENEMIES MAY SOMETIMES HAVE solutions for the problems they have caused in our lives because God uses them to do His bidding. Gideon and his men knew the victory was theirs because the enemy told them what would happen. God had given the enemy a dream and its interpretation and then made sure Gideon heard it. Gideon and his men entered the battle, blowing the trumpets, breaking pitchers to make lots of noise, and lifting their lamps as they shouted, "The sword of the Lord and Gideon!" Their enemy ran away, screaming and not even raising a sword. Israel did not face their enemies directly; they stood afar off, and God delivered the victory to them right where they stood.

WHEN GOD TOLD Gideon to send the 30,000 men home, He knew all along they would never face the enemy directly. He wanted the Israelites to understand that this victory was His alone. Gideon prevailed because he yielded his heart to the instructions of the Lord and was obedient, even though fearful at times. Gideon did not, however, allow his fear to stop him from persevering and faced his enemies, knowing God was with him. As a result, Gideon's life was forever changed. He went from being the least in his household to becoming a mighty man of valor, as the angel had prophesied over him during their first encounter.

HOW WILL YOU PRODUCE A HARVEST? You will create it through your obedience to God, even when doubtful about the outcome. Remember, God is the one who produces results in your life; you cannot be entirely successful on your own. In

Proverbs chapter 6, a father uses the example of an ant to tell his son how to produce a harvest—by working and refraining from sleeping too much.

THE ANT IS one of God's tiniest creatures and has no one to guide it. There is no overseer to give it instructions and no leader to lead it along the right path; yet during summertime, the ant gathers meat and goes to harvest and provides food for the winter season. This tiny creature hears and obeys the inner instructions of its Creator and prepares itself for whatever lies ahead, and so should we. No one can produce a harvest if they are lazy. An unsuccessful life is the result of a lack of preparation. The ant has the revelation from God that it is still required to have a productive life despite its size, and working is a part of God's plan for its life.

WE MUST FOLLOW the ant's example. You and I can only produce a harvest for our lives and others by yielding to God and doing the work He has assigned our hands to do. As we yield, we will become like ants, storing resources so we have a productive harvest and something to sustain us throughout our lives.

To Be Flexible and Pliable

A significant part of having a yielded heart is how flexible and pliable you are in the hands of God. Flexibility causes you to yield more readily to the instructions of the Lord, and it means you are sensitive, responsive, and manageable. Being pliable comes when you obey and submit to what God has for you to do, and speaks of a person who is obedient, submissive, and compliant. You will adapt to situations more readily as you apply these attributes. Being adaptable will produce a harvest of blessings in your life. As you adapt to what God has for you, you will become like the Prophet Isaiah and declare, "Here I am, Lord, send me."

IN THE YEAR that King Uzziah died I saw also the LORD sitting upon a throne, high and lifted up, and his train filled the temple. Above it stood the seraphims: each one had six wings; with twain he covered his face, and with twain he covered his feet, and with twain he did fly. And one cried unto another, and said, Holy, holy, holy is the LORD of hosts: the whole earth is full of his glory. And the posts of the door moved at the voice of him that cried, and the house was filled with smoke. Then said I, Woe is me! for I am undone; because I am a man of unclean lips, and I dwell in the midst of a people of unclean lips: for mine eyes have seen the King, the LORD of hosts. Then flew one of the seraphim unto me, having a live coal in his hand, which he had taken with the tongs from off the altar: And he laid it upon my mouth, and said, Lo, this hath touched thy lips; and thine iniquity is taken away, and thy sin purged. Also I heard the voice of the Lord, saying, Whom shall I send and who will go for us? Then said I, Here am I; send me.
—Isaiah 6:1-8 (KJV)

ISAIAH DISCOVERED THAT A YIELDED, flexible, and pliable heart required his participation. He received a revelation from God once his earthly king had died. Isaiah's eyes came wide open with the king's passing, and he saw the Lord clearly for the first time. Since nothing and no one was obstructing his view any longer, he could focus on the one true King. He discovered there could only be one king who reigns and rules in him, and it was the King of kings.

When he saw the Lord, he was amazed at what he saw. God was high and lifted up, and His train—His presence— filled the temple. Not only did His train fill the temple of worship, but it also filled Isaiah's physical temple and left him in awe and amazement. God's train covered everything in sight; it was all-encompassing. Isaiah saw the angels were yielded and pliable in the hands of the King as they worshipped the One who sits on the Throne.

The angels covered their faces with their wings as they called out to one another, "Holy, holy, holy is the Lord of hosts; the earth is filled with His glory." These angels are in awe of God even though they have been in His presence forever. They stop and worship God each time they behold his glory. These angels, also known as Seraphim, are called the burning ones. They are consumed with the presence of the Lord. Each time they see God, they cover their faces and feet because they cannot look upon His glory. Covering their faces means they recognize the holiness of God and are in such awe that they dare not look upon His face. Covering their feet means they acknowledge His purity and stand in the presence of the One who is beyond description.

WHEN ISAIAH REALIZED he was also in the presence of the Great I Am, he remembered who he was, a sinner who was unworthy of being in God's presence. He recalled not only his sins and that his mouth was unclean, but he also lived among unclean people. The scripture said when Isaiah remembered who he was, he almost came apart at the seams at the realization of being in the presence of the Holy God. As Isaiah recalled his sinful nature, one of the angels flew to him and removed his sins by touching his lips with a lump of live coal. Isaiah saw himself clearly for the first time in God's presence and could see his wickedness.

WHEN HIS EARTHLY KING REIGNED, Isaiah did not see his faults nor his sins as clearly, because they were not compared to God's standard of righteousness, only to man's. Isn't it amazing when we are surrounded by people who have similar problems, issues, or sins, we are unable to see ourselves or our sins? This happens because we subconsciously compare ourselves with others, and our sin often seems small in our eyes compared to theirs. Isaiah realized he was no better than any of his neighbors, and his sin condition was the same as theirs.

IT TAKES the presence of the Holy Spirit working in our hearts to point out our sins. This enables us to see our hearts clearly, so we can begin to deal with our issues. As we yield our hearts to Him, He begins purifying us by allowing the fire of His presence to burn away the sin in our lives. After the angel sanctified him, Isaiah heard the Lord saying, "Whom shall I send, and who will go for us?" God was looking for a messenger, and Isaiah responded to the call to be His messenger. He yielded to God and told God he was available and to send him. It is important to note he heard the voice of the Lord clearly after he had been cleansed and purified in the presence of the Lord.

AT TIMES, we do not hear the voice of God clearly, because

sin and other obstacles in our lives are blocking access to our hearing. Like Isaiah, we must look closely at our hearts and see ourselves through the eyes of God. We must then allow the Lord to deal with the things in our lives that concern Him. When Isaiah responded to the call of God and yielded his heart to Him, he became flexible and pliable in the hands of God. He was ready to be God's mouthpiece, and because his heart was yielded, he readily accepted God's assignment.

How YIELDED is your heart? Will you also answer "Yes," to God's call and "Yes," to His will? If you desire to be like God, to have a heart like His Son, and to be used by Him, you must yield your life entirely to Him. This includes your will, ways, plans, and destiny. Remember to surrender all!

CHAPTER 10
UNVEILING YOUR HEART

To reconnect to God, you must unveil your heart before Him by removing any masks you may be wearing. This means revealing what is hidden in you so God can reconnect you to His heart.

Some of us wear masks to conceal our thoughts, attitudes, and intentions. They are worn as a disguise and keep hidden the things we do not want to reveal. Not only do masks conceal what we do not want to show, but they can also hide things that need to be seen, such as our personalities, character, and intentions. Masks keep people from ascertaining who we are and where we are emotionally and spiritually. These masks conceal our thoughts, so most times, people cannot assist us in our trials or difficulties because they cannot discern our struggles. Our masks keep us from getting the help we need to overcome.

When wearing a mask, we present a false face to the world. A mask provides us with a covering; it acts as a shield. It is also a screen that locks us in and keeps others out of our lives. I venture to say that most of us have worn masks at various times, and some people have worn them for a lifetime. These masks have been our constant companions. Masks help us to present a pleasant face to the world. We wear them on the job, to church, and in our everyday lives, and sadly, we even wear them at home with our families. We are in disguise and often don't realize it, and unfortunately, neither do the people with whom we live, work, and play.

Think with me for a moment. Do you believe most people who know you know the real you? Do they know your frailties, concerns, needs, and desires, or have these been cloaked behind your mask? Many of us are so hidden behind our masks that we do not know ourselves. Here is what God's Word says to us.

"For the word of God is alive and powerful. It is sharper than the sharpest two-edged sword, cutting between soul and spirit, joint and marrow. It exposes our innermost thoughts and desires. Nothing in all creation is hidden from God. Everything is naked and exposed before his eyes, and he is the one to whom we are accountable." (Hebrews 4:12-13 NLT)

The Scripture is saying the All-Seeing, All-Knowing God sees our hearts and knows our thoughts. It is impossible to hide anything from Him since He is the Creator and can see all that is hidden. How we see ourselves and everything we think about and do is all laid naked before His eyes. He knows our plans. He sees what we meditate on and knows when we are happy and sad.

His Word is alive and powerful, and He uses it as a sword to cut away whatever has attached itself to our souls so we can live openly before Him. We can't hide ourselves or our hearts from God because He is all-knowing. God wants our thoughts exposed, so we can see what is in our hearts and begin to think in line with His will. He desires we think about things that are lovely, pure, and of a good report (Philippians 4:8). This will benefit our lives and bring His plans to fruition.

God is looking at our hearts to see our true intentions, and we must understand that one day we will have to give an account to Him for our decisions. Learn to be transparent with God, yourself, and with others. God loves you just as you are and does not want you to hide your true self from Him or the people in your life. He knows if people get to know the real you, they will love you as He does. He created you as you are; only you can accomplish the great things He has planned for your life.

A False Face

Some of us present a false face to the people around us and the world. We suppress who we are in hopes of attracting the right people or friends. Some people exaggerate their life stories and accomplishments and even adopt false identities because they do not believe who they are is significant or that they have what it takes to make a lasting impression. When we present a false face to others, we conceal our thoughts, emotions, and attitudes from scrutiny. This also keeps the real us, who we are, hidden from ourselves.

How often have you heard stories of people in relationships, but the other person does not get to know the real ones until months into the liaison? Others even claim they did not know the real person until they married and lived with them. In relationships, we tend to want to impress the person we are dating, so we're often on our best behavior and do not allow them to see our flaws and insecurities. Our personalities are hidden, and this keeps the person from knowing the real us and making a good decision about whether they wish to spend quality time with us.

It is impossible to keep your authentic self hidden for long. Sooner or later, who you are will surface, and then you will have to face yourself and deal with those you are trying to impress.

Keep in mind that each of us has areas in our lives that need to be refined, and these areas are refined as we grow and mature. We also have areas in our lives that reflect the beauty of God and who we are created to be in Him. Since you are made in God's image, you also have His nature and characteristics. As you look at the nature of God, you see a loving, caring, compassionate Father who does not withhold any good gifts from His children. He is merciful and tender, slow to anger, and abounding in love for us. Our God is powerful and all-knowing and has given us authority and power to be more than conquerors in this life. He is a God of great beauty who has created many beautiful things for us to enjoy. You are beautiful because He created you in His image.

When you do not present your authentic self to others, you keep them from discovering how special you are.

People throughout their lives have made bad choices that have corrupted their nature, so when you encounter them, they might be selfish, unforgiving, harmful, and even dangerous. They were not created evil but have allowed evil influences to taint their lives. These people often present a false face to the world, and you can become trapped in a relationship with them before discovering who they are, and they are not what they appear to be.

Please get to know people by spending time with their friends, relatives, and co-workers because they have been around them the longest, know them the best, and will give you insight into their character. People can't continue living a lie for an extended time without their true nature being revealed. As you get to know their friends, families, and associates, you will discover the real them. The Bible says there is safety in the multitude of counselors (Proverbs 11:14). Sometimes, we can be fooled into believing that what we see with our natural eyes represents the truth. The following story demonstrates this well.

When they arrived, Samuel took one look at Eliab and thought, "Surely this is the LORD's anointed!" But the LORD said to Samuel, "Don't judge by his appearance or height, for I have rejected him. The LORD doesn't see things the way you see them. People judge by the outward appearance, but the LORD looks at the heart."
—1 Samuel 16:6-7 (NLT)

146 JOAN E. MURRAY

God had appointed Saul as king over Israel, but Saul strayed from Him and neglected to follow His directives. God then took the kingdom back from Saul and told Samuel to appoint a new king over His people. Samuel was upset with the decision and was in mourning over Saul. God told him he had mourned long enough and to go to the house of Jesse because He had chosen a king from one of Jesse's sons.

When Samuel arrived, he took one look at Jesse's son, Eliab, who looked like a king, and automatically thought he was God's choice. Eliab's outer appearance fooled the prophet Samuel, and God had to correct his wrong assumption. God told Samuel not to judge by a person's appearance. Why? Because a person's physical appearance does not necessarily make them the right choice for an assignment. God told Samuel that He does not see things the way people see them; people look at outward appearance while He looks at a person's heart and qualifies them based on what is in their heart. This was an essential lesson for Samuel and us because we shouldn't judge only by appearance.

When God sent Samuel on the assignment, He could have told him the name of Jesse's son, whom He had chosen to be king, so that Samuel would have known right away, but God did not.

Jesse presented all his sons before Samuel, and God gave His verdict as Samuel looked at each one, and He said no to all seven. Samuel asked Jesse if these were all his sons because Samuel knew God had sent him to this house to anoint the new king. Jesse did not have seven sons; he had eight. However, he seemed to have forgotten about his last son, David, until Samuel questioned him. Jesse told Samuel his youngest was in the field, watching over the goats and the sheep. Samuel told him to send for David, and they would not sit down to eat until he arrived. Samuel knew without looking at the youngest son, David, that He was God's anointed one. Appearance no longer mattered.

The prophet Samuel discovered something important in this selection process. God does not select people based on their looks or other people's opinions.

He uses people based on what He knows is in their hearts, even when others may have disqualified them. David had been in the fields for years doing menial tasks, or so it seemed, but God was using this time to train, prepare, and develop his character so he would be an effective king for His people. David's father and brothers might have forgotten where he was, but God had not. God knew where David was in terms of his physical location and the alignment of his heart to God's heart. At the right time, God plucked him out of obscurity and brought him to the forefront.

God sees and knows the condition of every heart. He looks beyond the false face we present to the world and makes His decisions about our destinies based on what He finds in our hearts. God cannot be tricked or coerced into doing anything, and He wants us to be ourselves and allow people to get to know us. Step away from falsehood and allow people to discover the real you because they will be blessed by the uniqueness they find in you.

Shielded

We often place invisible barriers or shields around us when we wear masks. These barriers and shields are our armor and are meant to safeguard us against hurt and pain, but they are often ineffective. We use shields as defense mechanisms, hoping to keep us from disappointments, discouragement, and even despair, yet we still experience seasons of pain.

Some of you have viewed life from behind a screen because you are shielded from life. You cannot see out clearly, nor can anyone see you. Everything is blurry and out of focus in your life. These screens veil us from others and provide dividers that keep us from touching people's lives and keep others from touching us.

We live in a world filled with sin, so we will never be protected from the tragedies of life. Difficult situations will occur in our lives, families, jobs, and relationships; though painful, they present opportunities for us to grow and develop. Although people have used shields for centuries to protect themselves during war and tried other ways of safeguarding and shielding themselves from tragedies, God is our only true shield and defense.

But the LORD watches over those who fear him, those who rely on his unfailing love. He rescues them from death and keeps them alive in times of famine. We put our hope in the LORD. He is our help and our shield. In him our hearts rejoice, for we trust in his holy name. Let your unfailing love surround us, LORD, for our hope is in you alone.

—Psalm 33:18-22 (NLT)

Over time, you may have come to realize there is no safety outside of the protection of the Lord. God has become many people's shield and buckler and their only defense in times of trouble. He is constantly watching over those who revere Him and who rely on the unfailing love He has poured into their hearts. God knows the protections we have drawn around ourselves to shield us from life's difficulties are not strong enough to keep us safe. We must reconnect to Him and realign our hearts to His to be at peace during the chaos. He is our keeper! He watches over us day and night. God is our only hope, shield, and defense during famine, earthquakes, strife, and heartache. Our hearts can rest safely in His care because His love is always available, and He will protect us as He comforts us.

We have spent much time and effort trying to safeguard our hearts from hurts and pains, but the best thing we can do is reconnect our hearts to God's heart and allow Him to work His plans through us. God's eyes are on those who fear, honor, and love Him, and He keeps His focus on those whose hope is in Him alone. He is the only one who can deliver you from your trials, past and present because your shield is ineffective in providing the necessary protection.

As you reconnect to God and put your confidence in Him, He will see you through every trial. Psalm 3 gives us some explicit promises.

O LORD, I have so many enemies; so many are against me. So

many are saying, God will never rescue him!" But you, O LORD, are a shield around me; you are my glory, the one who holds my head high. I cried out to the LORD and he answered me from his holy mountain. I lay down and slept, yet I woke up in safety, for the LORD was watching over me. I am not afraid of ten thousand enemies who surround me on every side. Arise, O LORD! Rescue me, my God. Slap all my enemies in the face! Shatter the teeth of the wicked! Victory comes from you, O LORD. May you bless your people.
—Psalm 3:1-8 (NLT)

GOD IS YOUR SHIELD; He is the glory and lifters your head. If your head is bowed, He will lift you so you can rejoice in Him again. You are shielded by Him and are wrapped in His amazing care!

Unveiling our Hearts

Becoming like Jesus and truly living for Him means we must unveil our hearts to Him, so He can reveal whatever needs to be addressed to us.

You and I must put away the many masks we wear, which have camouflaged our authentic personalities, so we can embrace who we were born to become. I know you have seen people at masquerade parties wearing masks that covered most of their faces; because their faces were covered, you could not get a clear picture of their actual appearance. If they had a need and did not verbalize it, it would be hard to discern what they needed because you couldn't ascertain where they were.

ON MANY OCCASIONS, I have asked people how they are doing, and their replies have been, "I am blessed by the Lord." The Lord indeed blesses them, but in further conversation with them and others, I discovered they were going through some trying and challenging times. Their words were not an accurate indication of how they felt or how they were doing now. We all make positive confessions because the Bible tells us to call those things not as they were (Romans 4:17). The Scripture, however, does not suggest we ignore the issues in our lives. When necessary, we should seek help or advice from those who can assist us. The desire to be seen as blessed and prosperous can make it difficult for you to get the help you need.

GOD DESIRES to free you before the enemy severely damages your life, but people must know you need support. When Samuel saw Jesse's son, Eliab, he thought this one looked good. He has it all together. Everything seems to be going well for him. Samuel didn't realize that, like many of us, Eliab had his problems. Eliab looked good to the natural eyes, but God, who sees beyond the natural realm, saw something in his heart that disqualified him for service in the kingdom.

DURING ONE OF my unemployment stints, I learned something valuable. Some people may need to know when you are in a crisis so that they can help you. However, others are sensitive to God's voice and can hear Him clearly when He instructs them to assist. I had searched diligently for a job but had no success. I was always at church and, from my appearance, looked as if I was prosperous and living in abundance, even though I was financially strapped. While nothing was wrong with taking care of me and presenting my best despite being unemployed, my appearance presented a false impression to those around me. Shortly after I found a job, a lady approached me. She had learned I had been unemployed for some time. She said the Lord had told her several months before to give me five dollars, but she didn't. She did not realize that God knew my needs and that the five dollars would have helped my situation. She looked at my outward appearance and decided I did not need it because everything seemed well. She did not obey the instructions from the Lord to give me the five dollars.

I AM NOT SUGGESTING we broadcast our needs to everyone we meet. Nor do I advocate we ask people for financial help. I believe God is our provider. We can certainly share our struggles with people and seek help through prayer and counseling. Our transparency will help us connect with those who may have the answers. I encourage you not to misrepresent where you are in your walk of faith. Understand that God is available to help you and will also provide help through those who hear and obey Him.

Sometimes in our walk of faith, we want to shield ourselves or hide from life's difficulties, but it is not always possible. The word Simeon gave to Mary, the mother of Jesus, supports this.

AND, behold, there was a man in Jerusalem, whose name was

Simeon: and the same man was just and devout, waiting for the
consolation of Israel: and the Holy Ghost was upon him. And it was
revealed unto him by the Holy Ghost, that he should not see death,
before he had seen the Lord's Christ. And he came by the Spirit into
the temple: and when the parents brought in the child Jesus, to do
for him after the custom of the law, then took he him up in his arms,
and blessed God, and said, Lord, now lettest thou thy servant depart
in peace, according to your word: for mine eyes have seen thy
salvation, which thou hast prepared before the face of all people; a
light to lighten the Gentiles, and the glory of thy people Israel. And
Joseph and his mother marveled at those things which were spoken
of him. And Simeon blessed them, and said unto Mary his mother,
Behold, this child is set for the fall and rising again of many in
Israel; and for a sign which shall be spoken against; (Yea, a sword
shall pierce through thy own soul also,) that the thoughts of many
hearts may be revealed.
—Luke 2:25-35 (KJV)

SIMEON WAS AN OLDER man who had a promise from God
that he would not see death until he met the Son of God. At
the right time, the Spirit of God led him to the temple, so this
meeting with Jesus could occur. Simeon was given a
prophetic word that had to be delivered to Joseph and Mary,
and it was a word of revelation about what was to come. The
word was clear; Jesus would cause the fall and rise of many
in Israel, and He did. Many people would speak against him,
and a sword pierced Mary's soul.

JOSEPH AND MARY did not understand the prophecy, but it
later manifested in their lives. Mary endured many difficult

days as she watched Jesus being accused, abused, and tried for crimes He did not commit. A sword pierced her heart as she watched Him crucified like a common criminal. She could not help Him as she stood at Golgotha's hill and listened to the nails being driven into His broken body. She could not shield Him, protect Him, or hide Him, and her heart was pierced through and through.

THE JEWS HAD JESUS CRUCIFIED, not because He had done anything wrong, but because His actions and the miracles He performed showed them He was the Son of God, and they refused to believe this. They chose to silence His voice by killing Him, or so they thought. Through the pages of the Bible and Christians around the world, His voice has been ringing out for centuries. Each time Jesus was in the presence of the Jews, His actions and Words pierced their hearts and caused them to be uncomfortable because of the evil in them. He unveiled their hearts to them, as Stephen did, and since they did not like what they saw, they killed the Messenger, not believing God had sent Him to redeem mankind.

Mary allowed God to see what was clearly in her heart as she watched her Son's death on the cross. Even though Mary's heart was pierced, she had no choice but to allow God to finish what He planned for her Son. She experienced the pain of separation and the anguish of His suffering as she watched Him being dishonored and rejected by the people He came to serve; yet, all she could do was pray and trust God. Her heart was unveiled, and God had a clear view of whether she would be bitter toward Him for allowing this evil to happen or whether she would remember her words to

Him when the angel came with the news of Jesus' impending birth, "Be it unto me according to your word" (Luke 1:38 KJV). Mary stood strong, and God gave her victory when Jesus rose from the dead.

YOU AND I must open our hearts to God, no matter how painful the unveiling might be. We must be willing to remove our masks so He can mend the broken places in our hearts. We must see ourselves as we are so God can begin to remake us into the image of His Son. Unlike some Israelites, we must see our desperate need for the Savior and accept His forgiveness and deliverance. Remember, when you unveil your heart by removing the masks you wear, you will also help others become free.

CHAPTER 11
BENEFITS OF A RECONNECTED HEART

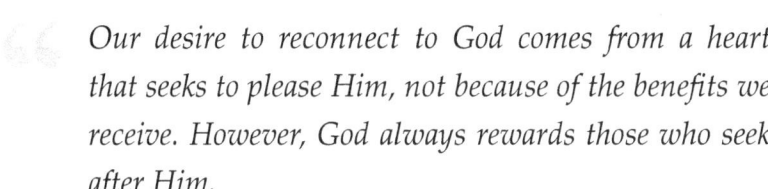

Our desire to reconnect to God comes from a heart that seeks to please Him, not because of the benefits we receive. However, God always rewards those who seek after Him.

We benefit from staying in close, intimate fellowship with Him. You and I reap numerous benefits from our relationship with Jesus Christ. We experience love in its most profound form, find joy even amid sorrow, obtain peace when there is chaos around us, walk in divine health and prosper even as our soul prospers, and experience the blessings of being children of the King. God seeks to shower us with the many blessings that Jesus died to provide for us. Jesus came and died not only to save us and give us a wonderful place to spend eternity but also, so we can become more than conquerors through Him in this life. As you study the Word of God, you will discover it contains thousands of promises for the believer.

GOD'S WORD is filled with demonstrations of His love and sacrifice on our behalf. In chapter one of this book, we talked about the intimate fellowship Adam and Eve had with God and how they had opportunities to meet with Him face-to-face each day. What a tragedy it was when they lost their connection with Him because of sin.

JESUS CAME, so you and I could once again have one-on-one communion and fellowship with our Creator. God loves us, and we are a part of His family. You receive many benefits when you are a part of a healthy family unit. As part of God's family, I want us to look at a few of the benefits we receive because we are His.

Love

FOR GOD so loved the world that he gave his one and only Son, that whoever believes in him shall not perish but have eternal life.
—John 3:16 (NIV)

THE ONE WHO does not love does not know God, for God is love. By this the love of God was manifested in us, that God has sent His only begotten Son into the world so that we might live through Him. In this is love, not that we loved God, but that He loved us and sent His Son to be the propitiation for our sins. Beloved, if God so loved us, we also ought to love one another. No one has seen God

at any time; if we love one another, God abides in us, and His love is
perfected in us.
—1 John 4:8-12 (NASB)

But God demonstrates His own love toward us, in that while we
were yet sinners, Christ died for us.
—Romans 5:8 (NASB)

No, in all these things we are more than conquerors through him
who loved us. For I am convinced that neither death nor life, neither
angels nor demons, neither the present nor the future, nor any
powers, neither height nor depth, nor anything else in all creation,
will be able to separate us from the love of God that is in Christ
Jesus our Lord.
—Romans 8:37-39 (NIV)

Let me share something noteworthy with you. When you read the Scriptures, you can make them personal by including your name in each verse with a promise for your life. The above Scriptures tell us that God loves us (including your name) and that He gave His only Son for you.

Love motivated God's gift. The love of the Father for us, His children, caused God to give His only Son to reunite us with Him. In my book, **Called and Chosen for Destiny**, I shared how Jesus became the ultimate sacrifice and how He relinquished all His glory and splendor when He descended from His throne to bring us new life.

The Father demonstrated His great love for us by giving,

and the Son showed His great love for us by dying. This love is God's amazing agape love, and despite our frailties, God still pours His love into our hearts. We have never experienced a love like this before and will never experience it in any human relationships. This love is unconditional and unchanging. Even when we are unlovable or neglect to do what is loving and honorable toward God, His love is constant and will not cause us to be ashamed. This unselfish love comes from God, rescuing us when we are lost. Love never abandons us and keeps pursuing us until we are once again wrapped in His loving and protective arms. God loves us so profoundly that He wants no one to perish but all to have eternal life.

First John 4 tells of God's love for us and encourages us to love as He does. The scriptures say if you do not love, you do not know God because God is love.

When you think of love, the first picture that should come to mind is a picture of God because He embodies love in its most profound form. The greatest love you and I will ever experience is not that we love God but that He loves us, and because of the richness of His love, we are then able to love one another. When God's love dwells richly in our hearts, it causes us to see others through His eyes and to love them as He loves them. In our love walk, the goal is for us to love unconditionally, to love despite what we feel, to love when a person seems impossible to love, and to have the willingness to lay down our lives for others as Jesus did -- this is the power of love.

WHILE WE WERE dead in sin, God demonstrated His love for us. He reached down from heaven and plucked us out of the grip of sin that was set up to enslave us throughout eternity. He sent Jesus to the cross, knowing the horrific death He would suffer because only through the shed blood of His innocent Lamb, Jesus, could we be forgiven and set free.

Have you ever experienced the richness of God's love for you? Maybe it was at a time in your life when nothing was lovable about you, but you discovered He continued to love you and desired to spend quality time with you. He looked beyond your sin and shame and embraced you, never once caring that you were covered with filth. He loved you so deeply that He pulled you out of the pit and brought you back into wholeness and a right relationship with Him.

IN ROMANS 8, we see that nothing will ever be able to separate us from the love of God. No tribulation, distress, persecution, famine, trouble, or war—nothing—can cause God to stop loving you and reaching out to you. God has made you a conqueror, so amid crisis, you can be victorious and triumph over the enemy through the power of the Holy Spirit and the love of God. God loves us so much! His Word declares neither death, nor life, angels, principalities, powers, the present things nor the things to come, nor height, nor depth, and no creature will ever be able to separate us from the love of God which He has poured out for us through Christ Jesus.

GOD's amazing love will cause you to know beyond a shadow of a doubt that no matter how many struggles you have endured, how long it has taken Him to move in your situation, or how tough life may seem, He is always with you. As you reconnect your heart to Him, He will pour His love into you until it overflows from your life and encompasses everyone around you. *Love is waiting for you. Will you reconnect today?*

Joy

I heard a song many years ago that speaks to us about joy. It reminded me joy needs to be a significant part of a Believer's life. The joy God gives can sustain us when our life seems to be falling apart.

This song encouraged me to hold on to joy, hide it deep in my heart, and never let go, even when the storms are raging out of control in my life. As children, I believe some of you learned many songs about joy, and they speak volumes about how you and I maintain our hope and peace during difficult times. Joy must be so securely embedded in our hearts that nothing can dislodge it. Sometimes, we have been joyless because the circumstances and situations of life have pushed the joy out of our hearts.

A BENEFIT of belonging to God is having and maintaining the joy of the Lord in our lives. His joy gives us strength and sustains us! His joy fills our hearts with hope and keeps us from sinking into despair! His joy motivates us to keep smiling and to keep pressing onward! Have you faced circumstances that have robbed you of your joy? It might have been the loss of a job, health crisis, relationship problem, or tragedy in your family; these things were sent to steal the joy of the Lord out of your heart. When the joy robber came, it was after your strength because the Scripture says the joy of the Lord is your strength (Nehemiah

8:10). If you have no strength, you cannot fight and gain victory.

THE BIBLE ABOUNDS with Scriptures about joy because joy is necessary for you to live a healthy and productive life, and joy produces the health you need to live in peace. We will explore a few Scriptures on joy, so you can find the strength to live each day in the fullness of joy and victory.

YOU WILL SHOW me the path of life; In Your presence is fullness of joy; At your right hand are pleasures forevermore.
—Psalm 16:11 (NKJV)

WEEPING may endure for a night, but joy comes in the morning.
—Psalm 30:5 (NKJV)

THOSE WHO SOW in tears shall reap in joy.
—Psalm 126:5 (NKJV)

THESE THINGS I have spoken to you, that My joy may remain in you, and that your joy may be full.
—John 15:11 (NKJV)

WHERE DO YOU FIND JOY? In the presence of the Lord! One of the benefits of being a child of God is when you reconnect to Him and tap into a wellspring of joy. In God's presence is fullness of life and fullness of joy. His joy enables you to face difficulties and overcome them while still maintaining your peace.

As you reconnect to God and rest in His presence, you

will experience joy from connecting to Him. The joy of knowing you are welcome in His company at any time and in any circumstances releases you to find rest under His wings. God understands the trials the enemy brings against you are designed to keep you from experiencing His joy, which will help you maintain a healthy immune system. He wants your joy to be complete and overflowing, so you can be well and live well.

I have a friend and co-laborer in the gospel, Gloria, who exemplifies a joy-filled life. As a result, she is one of the healthiest people I know.

A STORM AROSE while we were ministering and conducting missions in Belize, Central America, in October 2010. During the storm, Gloria was joyful. Her joy was so contagious, the team, and I laughed and rejoiced continually, even as the wind and rain pounded our hotel. She told jokes, danced on her toes, and had us wholly wrapped up in the joy of being in the center of God's will on this mission trip; we did not have a moment of fear or dread during what turned out to be a hurricane. We could minister and be the hands and feet of Jesus to the fearful people in the hotel and those who needed hope and help after the storm.

Gloria had incredible joy, which overflowed and filled our hearts. This caused us to trust in God's faithfulness to see us through the assignment He had given us in Belize, even during and after the storm.

IN THE BOOK OF PSALMS, David constantly speaks about joy because he faced many situations designed to rob him of his joy. Once God appointed him as Saul's replacement, he spent many years on the run and hiding because of Saul's jealousy. Saul wanted to kill David because he was appointed the new king.

David had to stay connected to God and spend time in His presence to maintain his joy. He knew the enemy wanted to steal his strength by robbing him of his joy, and the only way he would ascend to the throne and become king of Israel was to maintain his joy and strength until God removed Saul. He had to stay connected to the joy of his life, God, because only in this connection could he fulfill his destiny and enjoy the benefits of peace during the battles. David reminds us that even though "...weeping may endure for a night, joy comes in the morning" (Psalm 30:5 NKJV).

DAVID UNDERSTOOD things always appear to be worse during the night. If he could get to the light of day, he would see more clearly and realize that every problem has a solution. What may seem impossible at night will become possible when the light of God is shining on it.

The same holds for you as well. Although David experienced seasons when he wept and sought God for the restoration of his joy, God was always there to safeguard him in the difficult journeys that were designed to rob him of his destiny. David tells us, "… Those who sow in tears shall reap in joy" (Psalm 126:5 NJKV).

What things have you wept over? What difficulty has kept you sad, depressed, and joyless? You can be assured that the seeds of your tears will bring about a harvest of joy in your life, whatever caused you to pour out tears before God.

Psalm 56:8 is one of my favorite Scriptures because it tells us how precious our tears are to God. "You keep track of all my sorrows. You have collected all my tears in your bottle. You have recorded each one in your book" (NLT). God is aware of every tear you have shed. He has documented each one and has wept with you over the devastations in your life. He keeps a record of your tears, and I am convinced that one day you will get to see this bottle He has kept with the evidence of your sorrows. I believe they will become precious jewels for you.

To MAINTAIN and retain your joy, you must experience a reconnection to God. Jesus said, "These things I have spoken to you, that My joy may remain in you, and that your joy may be full" (John 15:11 NKJV). What has Jesus declared in John 15:7-16 that will keep us filled with joy?

Staying connected to the Vine:

Allowing His Word to remain in our hearts.
He loves us even as the Father has loved Him.
Remaining in His love.
Obeying His commandments.
Loving one another in the same way, He loves us.
Being willing to lay down our lives for our friends.
Becoming His friend.
Understanding that He has chosen us.
Producing fruit so the Father can bless us.

Do you want joy, absolute and incredible joy? Get reconnected to the heart of God and experience an overflow of His joy.

Peace

One of the greatest needs of our hearts is to be at peace. Peace brings comfort and joy to our souls. Along with the love and joy God gives us, He also desires we live our lives abounding with His peace.

Without peace, we cannot function in our homes, jobs, or relationships. In my book, *Winning in The Battles Of Life*, I shared the spiritual armor God provided for the Believer. One piece of this armor is the 'shoes of peace' that God has given to steady us during the battles. Whenever our peace is interrupted, it causes stress and worries in our lives. Stress and worry can lead to sickness and disease, which is one of the main reasons we must remain peaceful no matter our difficulties.

When you reconnect your heart and life to God, the situations designed to nullify your peace will not affect you as intensely because God enables you to rest in His peace as you stay connected to Him. God has given us His peace as one of the fruits of the Spirit. The fruit of peace is a part of the covenant plan God has for the Believer, and as we stay connected to Him, peace will become paramount in our hearts and lives. The Word of God is filled with promises of peace, and He has made it possible for us to be at peace by finding rest in His care.

*YOU WILL KEEP him in perfect peace, whose mind is stayed on You,
because he trusts in You.*
—Isaiah 26:3 (NKJV)

*THEREFORE, since we have been justified through faith, we have
peace with God through our Lord Jesus Christ.*
—Romans 5:1 (NIV)

*THESE THINGS I have spoken unto you, that in me ye might have
peace. In the world ye shall have tribulation: but be of good cheer; I
have overcome the world.*
—John 16:33 (KJV)

*PEACE I leave with you; My peace I give to you; not as the world
gives do I give to you. Let not your heart be troubled, neither let it
be afraid.*
—John 14:27 (NKJV)

*BE CAREFUL FOR NOTHING; but in everything by prayer and
supplication with thanksgiving let your requests be made known
unto God. And the peace of God, which passeth all understanding,
shall keep your hearts and minds through Christ Jesus.*
—Philippians 4:6-7 (KJV)

*LET the peace of Christ rule in your hearts, to which indeed you
were called in one body; and be thankful.*
—Colossians 3:15 (NASB)

These are only a few Scriptures that speak to us about the peace God desires to give us. As we keep our minds and hearts focused on Jesus, His peace is perfected in us. This means peace will guide and help to stabilize us when things are not working in our favor.

JESUS GUARANTEES us peace because the Scriptures say we have been justified by faith in Him. As we tap into His power and find rest for our emotions, we will not be troubled or afraid when the cares of life crowd in on us. Jesus understands that we will face trials and tribulations in the world, so He has given us peace to bring us through. We are assured of His peace because He has overcome the world and made us overcomers through Him.

Throughout His tenure on earth, Jesus talked much about peace. He wants us to live free of anxiety, to pray about everything that concerns us, and to have our hearts filled with thanksgiving. It is difficult for the enemy to dislodge God's peace from our hearts when we are thankful. Jesus has given us His peace, not the peace of the world. His sustaining peace will keep our hearts from being troubled and keep fear from hounding us.

WE HAVE BEEN GIVEN a choice to allow the peace of God to rule or not rule in our hearts. During a crisis, we must tap into God's peace. We must remember His peace is available because we are connected to Him. We may sometimes lack peace because of the people around us. Have you ever had a boss who is cranky, demanding, and disruptive to your serenity? Since many of us spend most of our waking hours on the job, this can make for a stressful life. I have had such a boss, and the lack of peace in my work environment created some health problems. I would confess the peace of God over myself daily but had difficulty maintaining it amid harsh words and criticism.

One day, a turnaround came when I realized that one of God's promises is that wherever the soles of my feet tread, the land is mine (Joshua 1:3). Since I am a believer, that promise belongs to me, and I began to speak it. I was the first person to arrive at the office each day, so I began to pray over the office my boss used and for peace in our environment.

AFTER PRAYING like this over time, I discovered I could remain at peace in the face of her irritability. When the other staff members asked me what mood she was in, I would tell them it did not matter as they were not there to please her but to work 'as unto the Lord'. The atmosphere in the office began to change because I changed and was no longer allowing the devil to rob me of my peace. My boss also noticed the things she did and said no longer moved me from my position of peace. When corrections were justified, I complied, and when they were not, I spoke up. Things began to change because I started operating in what I knew and who I was—a child of God with His benefit of peace.

You must tap into the peace God has provided because, without peace, life becomes difficult and, in some cases, unbearable. Peace is necessary not only on the job but also in your home.

MANY YEARS AGO, I lived in an apartment complex where the neighbors above me fought constantly. This stressed me out even though there was peace in my own home. I spoke to the management company about the situation, but it did not change, so I took matters into my own hands and spoke directly to the couple. The couple calmed down for a short time, but they were soon back to arguing again. I decided to pray, and within a few months, they moved out, and the environment was peaceful again. Guard your peace in whatever way you can because, without peace, life can become stressful and difficult. Jesus came to reconnect you to your Source of peace, and God wants you to have peace in your souls and rest from the burdens of life. I invite you to reconnect to your Source of peace today!

Health

When you are at peace, it is easier to walk in divine health. As joy emanates from you, your health springs forth. You will have a healthy and fulfilling life when you love as God loves you.

Jesus bore thirty-nine stripes on His back, and He suffered so we might be healed. We do not have to live with sickness and disease. When we reconnect to God, He will teach us how to allow His Word to become medicine for our lives. We serve a God who heals! God is interested not only in healing our bodies but also in our emotions. He wants to provide holistic care for our lives—spirit, soul, and body.

Our connection to God gives us the preventive care needed to combat any sickness and disease attack. A heart of thankfulness and gratitude goes a long way in keeping us healthy and is a massive part of our preventive care plan.

Taking care of not only our spirit man but also our physical bodies through regular exercise and healthy eating will help to combat the onslaught of sickness and disease.

I HAVE several friends in their seventies who are healthy and strong and can run circles around many of us who are half their age. They are healthy and strong because they are connected to God and have daily communion and fellowship with Him. They take care of themselves and ascribe to the Word of God, which tells them God desires them to live in divine health and prosper. The Word is their lifeline, and they stay in its pages. As a result, they are healthy and doing more for God now than when they were younger. The latter part of their lives is more incredible than the former (Job 42:12).

GOD WANTS you to be healthy and strong. He allowed Jesus to suffer horrific pain to provide us with healing. Jesus suffered great agony to free us from the bonds of sin and release us from the grip of sickness and disease. As you have studied the Word, you have discovered numerous healing Scriptures that have become your favorites when the enemy attacks your health. The Scriptures below are some of my favorites.

SURELY HE HATH BORNE our griefs, and carried our sorrows: yet we did esteem him stricken, smitten of God, and afflicted. But he was wounded for our transgressions; he was bruised for our iniquities: the chastisement of our peace was upon him; and with his stripes we are healed.
—Isaiah 53:4-5 (KJV)

Then they cry unto the LORD in their trouble, and he saveth them out of their distresses. He sent his word, and healed them, and delivered them from their destructions.
—Psalm 107:19-20 (KJV)

Bless the LORD, O my soul: and all that is within me, bless his holy name. Bless the LORD, O my soul, and forget not all his benefits: Who forgiveth all thine iniquities; who healeth all thy diseases; Who redeemeth thy life from destruction; who crowneth thee with lovingkindness and tender mercies;

Who satisfieth thy mouth with good things; so that thy youth is renewed like the eagle's.
—Psalm 103:1-5 (KJV)

For I will restore health unto thee, and I will heal thee of thy wounds, saith the LORD.
—Jeremiah 30:17 (KJV)

As you read and declare these Scriptures over your life, you can tap into the promises, and provisions God has made for your health and well-being. He wants you healed and free from the grip of pain. He took our sorrows and was wounded so we would be healed. God's Word is a powerful antidote for keeping us healthy.

Psalm 107 says He sent His Word and healed you. This means the Word will bring healing to your body when you speak the Scriptures God gives you to combat sickness and disease. The Word is packed with power, and when you speak the Word over your situation, it infuses it with life. The Scripture says God does not forget His benefits to His children, and one of His benefits is good health. God promised He would pardon us and forget our sins, and He never forgets His promise of healing for our lives. As we stay in close connection with Him, our healing will spring forth speedily.

WHEN YOU PLANT the Word of God deeply into your heart and act on the knowledge that He promised to restore health to you and heal all your wounds, He will precisely do that. I encourage you to think about the many times the Lord has provided for you, whether it was healing, joy, peace, love, or finances. Then remember He is the same yesterday, today, and forever; He will never change. His promise of healing is as sure as the dawn, and as you take His promises and speak them over your situation, they must manifest in your life.

SPEAKING the Word of God over your circumstances guarantees a harvest in your life because His Word will never return to Him empty. Isaiah 55 says, "As the rain and the snow come down from heaven, and do not return to it without watering the earth and making it bud and flourish so that it yields seed for the sower and bread for the eater, so is my word that goes out from my mouth: It will not return to me empty but will accomplish what I desire and achieve the purpose for which I sent it" (Isaiah 55:10-11). God's Word is pregnant with life and will birth something of great value in your heart. Reconnect with God today and stay healthy!

Prosperity

We cannot discuss the benefits of reconnecting to God without discussing how God desires to prosper us. Throughout the Scriptures, beginning in Genesis, you will find the abundance of God's prosperity for His children. Adam and Eve were placed in a garden overflowing with God's blessings.

ABRAHAM WAS RICH IN CATTLE, silver, and gold. Jacob stole Esau's birthright and was blessed with a large family and cattle. Joseph became the second in command in Egypt and gained incredible wealth because God used his gift of interpreting dreams to open huge doors of opportunity for him. Our forefathers were blessed and prosperous because they obeyed God. God always rewards obedience.

WHEN YOU AND I reconnect our hearts to God and begin to do things His way, our reward will also be an abundant harvest in our lives. You must understand He is a loving Father who dearly loves His children and desires to bless them continuously. God is unlike many earthly fathers who sometimes will not even provide for their children. No, He instructs us in His Word to leave an inheritance for our children's children; therefore, if God instructs mere men to provide for their children, how much more will He provide for us?

AT TIMES, due to our financial struggles, we may think God does not care if we live from paycheck to paycheck. At other times, we may feel God is not concerned about whether we have enough food to sustain ourselves. We sometimes base our reasoning on the circumstances we see around us, such as hunger and starvation in many nations, and attribute these dire conditions to God.

God has created a world filled with an abundant harvest for all His creation. There is ample supply to meet mankind's needs, but corrupt and greedy men and women have robbed many of the provisions meant for others. God wants you to know there is an abundant harvest connected to living in the right relationship with Him. It is not only a harvest of spiritual and material blessings to enrich your life. If you lack the necessary means to take care of yourself, God has provided an answer through someone else. He has given abilities and resources to many people to take care of the needs of the poor, widows, and orphans.

IN OUR WORK on the mission field, locally and internationally, we provide food, clothing, toys, and gifts to those in need. We can do this because of people who are generous and have the desire to help those who are less fortunate. I believe God speaks to many people's hearts to give to those in need, but we are so wrapped up in the material things of this world that often, we do not hear Him. We will not give to meet the needs if we do not listen to Him. Sadly, we often miss the opportunity to be the hands and feet of Jesus to a dying, depraved humanity.

WHEN GOD SPEAKS to our hearts, but we do not obey His instructions to meet the needs of others, they are left without the necessary means to take care of themselves. I know in our country (USA), the welfare system more than provides for some who are capable of providing for themselves, and many abuse our tax dollars. However, some people in our country and other countries need the financial blessings God has poured into many of His children's lives.

AS WE RECONNECT our hearts to God, He begins to share His heart and concerns about people. One of His concerns is that many live below the poverty line, even though He has given us abundant wealth on the earth. The question must be asked—what is the state of our hearts that we would not seek to help others as we prosper? As chapter two of this book mentions, we all have heart issues that must be checked, passed through God's microscope, and dealt with by Him. Until God can cause us to see the condition of our hearts clearly, we will not be moved by His compassion to help others.

WHEN JESUS LIVED ON EARTH, He demonstrated a heart overflowing with compassion. Once the disciples wanted Him to send the crowd away to get food, but He told them to feed the multitude. Listen to this story and examine the disciples' hearts toward the people who were in need.

WHEN JESUS HEARD what had happened, he withdrew by boat privately to a solitary place. Hearing of this, the crowds followed him on foot from the towns. When Jesus landed and saw a large crowd, he had compassion on them and healed their sick. As evening approached, the disciples came to him and said, "This is a remote place, and it's already getting late. Send the crowds away, so they can go to the villages and buy themselves some food." Jesus replied, "They do not need to go away. You give them something to eat." "We have here only five loaves of bread and two fish," they

answered. "Bring them here to me," he said. And he directed the people to sit down on the grass. Taking the five loaves and the two fish and looking up to heaven, he gave thanks and broke the loaves. Then he gave them to the disciples, and the disciples gave them to the people. They all ate and were satisfied, and the disciples picked up twelve basketfuls of broken pieces that were left over. The number of those who ate was about five thousand men, besides women and children.
—Matthew 14:13-21 (NIV)

IN THIS SCRIPTURE, you can see Jesus' compassion for the people and His desire to provide for them. The disciples told Jesus the people were hungry, and they did not have food to feed them. They also offered Him what they thought was the right solution—to send the people into the villages so they could get something to eat. Jesus' response is very telling and challenging to all of us. "Don't send them away; you feed them." The disciples told Jesus all they had were five loaves and two fish. They looked from a natural perspective and could not see how this meager food supply could feed thousands of people. They had forgotten they were in the presence of the Miracle Worker.

I BELIEVE the disciples recognized the multitudes were with them all day and were possibly hungry. I also think the disciples felt compassion toward them. Their kindness, however, did not lead them to see they had the solution to the problem. They had some food but did not realize God could multiply it. They failed to understand God could use what they had, although it was a minuscule amount. Even after

Jesus told them to feed the people, they still did not realize He had equipped them to meet the needs. Jesus has also supplied us with what is necessary to meet the needs of those around us, but many of us still do not realize we have all it takes for the task.

AFTER JESUS TOOK the food and blessed it, He had the disciples serve the people. Jesus allowed them to be His hands and feet. He gave them the solution to the problem and the opportunity to be a blessing by serving. The disciples had the solution to take care of the needs of the people. We also have the solutions. When we feel compassion toward someone, we should take what we have, bless it, give thanks to God, and then expect Him to multiply it. God sees our desire to provide for those in need, and He will bless our efforts.

OVER THE PAST SEVERAL YEARS, I have seen God multiply the seeds He has given to our ministry to feed and clothe the thousands of people He has allowed us to care for because He will always honor those who seek to help the poor. The Bible says when you give to the poor, you are lending to the Lord (Proverbs 19:17). I believe when you lend to the Lord, God will repay you with interest. You are called to live a life of prosperity so that you can be a blessing to others. Prosperity means to grow, multiply, thrive, and flourish. As you reconnect your heart to God, His plan is for you to grow, multiply, thrive, and flourish in His presence. As these benefits manifest in your life, you will help others to experience their prosperity in God.

Here is what the Word says about your prosperity.

Misfortune pursues the sinner, but prosperity is the reward of the righteous.
—Proverbs 13:21 (NIV)

Commit to the LORD whatever you do, and your plans will succeed.
—Proverbs 16:3 (NIV)

He who keeps understanding shall prosper and find good.
—Proverbs 19:8 (AMP)

When the LORD blesses you with riches, you have nothing to regret.
—Proverbs 10:22 (CEV)

A generous man will prosper; he who refreshes others will himself be refreshed.
—Proverbs 11:25 (NIV)

But I will bless those who trust me. They will be like trees growing beside a stream - trees with roots that reach down to the water, and with leaves that are always green. They bear fruit every year and are never worried by a lack of rain.
—Jeremiah 17:7-8 (MSG)

THE THIEF COMES ONLY in order to steal and kill and destroy. I came that they may have and enjoy life, and have it in abundance (to the full, till it overflows).
—John 10:10 (AMP)

BELOVED, I pray that you may prosper in every way and [that your body] may keep well, even as [I know] your soul keeps well and prospers.
—3 John 1:2 (AMP)

AFTER READING THESE SCRIPTURES, do you see how much God desires to prosper you? As you search His Word, you will find numerous Scriptures, when acted upon, will cause you to have an abundant harvest, so you can live in prosperity, to the full, till it overflows!

IN READING THIS BOOK, I hope you have discovered which areas of your heart need to be reconnected to God. I pray you are more determined than ever to have intimate contact and fellowship with Him, which will cause your relationship to bloom and blossom. As you get and stay connected to God, I pray you will come to discover a greater and richer life in Him—a richness of life you have never experienced but always hoped to have in Him.

REMEMBER to reconnect your heart to God to experience His amazing love, joy, peace, health, and prosperity. Reconnection is the key to victory and a fulfilling life. May you enjoy the many benefits of reconnecting to God.

CONFESSION

Father, I know without Jesus, I am lost and without hope. I acknowledge You sent Jesus into the world to die for my sins. I believe He is Your Son, He was born of a virgin, and He died and then arose from the dead for my sins. I acknowledge I have sinned and fallen short of Your standards and ask You to forgive me.

I INVITE Jesus to come into my heart because the Bible says He is the only way, truth, and life, and no man comes to the Father but by Him. Father, I am coming to You in the precious name of Your Son, Jesus. I thank You now for saving me and setting me free, in Jesus' name.

Amen! (So be it).

I MUST PRAY

A GUIDE TO A POWERFUL PRAYER LIFE

JESUS PRAYED!

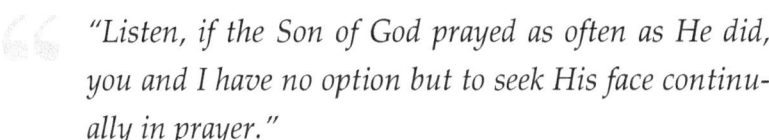 *"Listen, if the Son of God prayed as often as He did, you and I have no option but to seek His face continually in prayer."*

During the days of Jesus' life on earth, he offered up prayers and petitions with fervent cries and tears to the one who could save him from death, and he was heard because of his reverent submission. Son though he was, he learned obedience from what he suffered and, once made perfect, became the source of eternal salvation for all who obey him and was designated by God to be high priest in the order of Melchizedek (*Hebrews 5:7-10 – NIV*).

Throughout His time on earth, Jesus prayed continually. He sought the face of God often and taught us how to do the same. He stayed close to His Father through prayer. From the scriptures, we see He spoke with God in the morning, at mid-day, and night, and stayed in close fellowship and communion with Him. He was not limited by time or manmade rules about which was the best time of day to pray. He understood prayer was a MUST at any time. From His example we find Jesus prayed without ceasing, and so can we. His connection with God was vital to His life and His assignment for mankind. Prayer kept Him steady as He journeyed toward each assignment that would culminate into His final assignment—death on the cross. Prayer sustained Him amid all the fiery trials He faced. When the Jewish leaders tried to trap Him so they could accuse Him of blasphemy, Jesus was able to withstand them because He had prayed. While He was in the Garden of Gethsemane prior to His crucifixion, He prayed. In each moment of agony, He prayed, and God strengthened Him.

You can see Jesus recognized His need for prayer. We must come to the same understanding that prayer is a need that MUST be fulfilled in order for us to have victory over life's challenges. Throughout the Gospels (Matthew, Mark, Luke, and John), you see the many times Jesus prayed. In this chapter, I want to explore some of His prayers so you can gain wisdom concerning what He prayed about. My goal is that you will learn how to pray and what to pray for so you will get the same results as Jesus.

NOTES

1. Chapter 6 - Quotes from Mother Teresa

2. Chapter 9 - Story of Judson Van Deventer and Words to his song – All to Jesus I Surrender

ABOUT THE AUTHOR

Joan Murray is committed to helping people discover their destinies. She is the founder and CEO of Joan Murray Ministries and Seeds of Hope Worldwide Missions. Joan is dedicated to teaching, training, equipping, and helping people who are in various life struggles.

Joan is a minister, Bible teacher, author, and missionary. She has traveled extensively throughout the United States and internationally sharing the gospel message and serving the needs of the downtrodden. Joan currently resides in Houston, Texas.

If you would like to know more about Joan Murray Ministries or Seeds of Hope Worldwide Missions, please contact us at:

Joan Murray Ministries & Seeds Of Hope Worldwide
Missions
26340 FM 1736
Waller, TX 77848
281-398-2501
email: jmmcontactus@gmail.com
website: www.jemmuniquegift.com
website: www.joanmurrayministries.org

Changing Lives Through the Power and Truth of God's Word.

www.ingramcontent.com/pod-product-compliance
Lightning Source LLC
Chambersburg PA
CBHW062319120626
46546CB00013B/2083